Imagine

TOMMY SHERIDAN is Scotland's best-known socialist campaigner and was elected as a Member of the Scottish Parliament for Glasgow in 1999. Jailed for six months in 1992 for his opposition to the Poll Tax, the charismatic and controversial Sheridan has always been a thorn in the side of the Establishment.

ALAN McCOMBES is the editor of the *Scottish Socialist Voice* newspaper and was one of the pivotal figures in founding the Scottish Socialist Party. McCombes is widely regarded as one of the leading theoreticians of the Scottish Left.

Imagine

A Socialist Vision for the 21st Century

Tommy Sheridan and Alan McCombes

First published in Great Britain in 2000 by
Rebel Inc, an imprint of
Canongate Books Ltd, 14 High Street,
Edinburgh EH1 1TE

10 9 8 7 6 5 4 3 2 1

Rebel Inc series editor: Kevin Williamson
www.rebelinc.net

British Library Cataloguing-in-Publication Data
A catalogue record for this book is available on
request from the British Library

ISBN 1 84195 056 4

Typeset by Palimpsest Book Production Limited,
Polmont, Stirlingshire
Printed and bound by Omnia Books Ltd, Bishopbriggs, Glasgow.

Contents

PART THREE: POWER TO THE PEOPLE

PART FOUR: IMAGINE

Foreword

by Peter Mullan

I didn't want to write this. I'll be honest and say I did everything I could to avoid it. Not because I don't agree with what is written – I do.

I just hate the idea that my name is deemed necessary to endorse something as universal, as vital, as important, as socialism. Especially socialism in a Scottish context.

My name means fuck all. My own children don't even have my name! They have their mother's surname and that's not because we are separated (we've been together twelve years) but because I know to the core of my being that they are part of me as I am part of them and that's all that matters to me. The name, the label, is irrelevant.

Imagine – A Socialist Vision for the 21ˢᵗ Century, as created by Tommy and Alan, is their work, not mine and it can stand on its own. These are two highly intelligent, committed socialists, for whom I have the deepest respect and have known since I was a Young Socialist in the late 1970s. So if I were you I'd skip this bit and go straight to the first chapter.

For those of you who, for whatever reasons, want to know my opinion, I feel obliged to take note of historian E H Carr who said, 'Before you can understand history you must first understand the historian.' So as quickly as I can, I'll introduce myself.

I am any, one and very possibly none of the following: son of a nurse and a toolmaker, the brother of three sisters and four brothers, a pupil at Lourdes Primary, Our Lady of the Rosary, Lourdes Secondary, a Catholic (surprise, surfuckinprise), a paperboy, a grocer's assistant, a shelf stacker in the old Co-op in Paisley Road West, a baby-sitter for a neurosurgeon's weans, a labourer in a bed-making factory, a would-be playwright, a student, a check-out operator in the hypermarket, a residential care worker, a barman in the Viking Bar in Maryhill, a volunteer in a homeless unit in London, a disco dancer, a graduate of Glasgow Uni, a psychiatric patient at the Southern General Hospital, a film school reject, a prison visitor, a night porter, a drama worker in the Wine Alley, a researcher and tutorial assistant at Glasgow University, a drama worker for the WEA, a founder member of the Redheads, a sitcom writer, a professional actor, unemployed, an actor with Wildcat Theatre Co, an actor with the Tron Theatre Co, an anti-Poll-Tax campaigner, a television writer, unemployed, a father, a short film-maker, an orphan, a panic-attack sufferer, a flyophobe, a feature film-maker, an actor with awards attached, the guy in *The Steamie*, the guy wi' the rubber legs in *The Celtic Story*, the guy that stood next to Davy McKay in *Braveheart*, the big baldy bastard that wis in *Trainspotting*, that actor cunt that was in *My Name Is Orphans*.

So bearing all that in mind, here are my thoughts on this book. Like I said, it's been written by two men for whom I have THE DEEPEST REGARD. Reading the book, I found myself having to make the mental leap from ideals of socialism to the practicalities of how they may be applied in 21st-century Scotland. There are minor details I don't agree with, some I want to know more about, the vast majority I support completely.

It's a great feeling and a little daunting to map out the practice and means of a Scottish Socialist Republic. Great, because I honestly believe it's possible. Daunting because I honestly believe it's possible.

As a product of that none-too-subtle slavery that is known

as Western Capitalist Democracy, you're always conscious that socialist ideals will remain just and only that. An ideal. Something that can never actually be.

That the task is too great, the enemy too powerful. So let's rally around the odd issue, go on the occasional demo, attend the odd meeting and, when times are really hard, let's retreat to soap-opera socialism where every worker loves his mammy and every capitalist hates his da (but really their ma and da were lovers so we're aw brothers after ahhh).

The most exciting thing about this book is that it has the nerve to apply socialist principles to present-day Scotland. It presents a programme around which democracy can be applied. By reading it you can begin to take part in something genuinely revolutionary: a working, participatory Scottish Socialist Republic. A creation of our own.

Foreword

by William McIlvanney

Thanks to the widespread acceptance of monetarist theories in recent times, official political debate has been largely reduced to a kind of non-dialectical materialism. There has developed a tendency to judge a society by how much money it can generate, no matter how few bank accounts the bulk of that money comes to rest in. The pursuit of capital for its own sake has kicked up a drifting mist of pragmatism which has obscured from us our deeper aspirations, like fallout that deforms our dreams. The result has been to marginalise the importance of reconstructing society towards a more justly shared community of living.

One reason why I welcome this book is that it reinstates the demand for social justice at the centre of political debate, which is where it belongs. Social justice is not some optional extra which can be fitted in once we get our sums right. It is the very principle which will determine the rightness or wrongness of our sums.

It is heartening to see these authors start from this premiss. Chapter by chapter, the issues they cover will seem to map out terrain with which we are familiar but the angle of total commitment to social justice from which they view them may give us fresh perspectives. Certainly, in these writings, some things which contemporary attitudes might have taken for natural landmarks, as inevitable as mountains, can be seen as man-made excrescences, as avoidable as slagheaps.

It won't be necessary to agree with all the arguments here to see the validity of this book. What it most importantly does is to demand that we extend our concern beyond the efficiency of the economy towards the deeper purposes such efficiency might serve. It is an attempt, through a perception of where we are, to arrive at some sort of vision of where we might be.

Such vision was never more necessary than it is now, when many of our aspirations seem to have a horizon of about six inches. The idea of a just society is a bit like the Kraken. We have never found it but we can imagine it out there. If we can imagine it, we should keep looking. This book is still searching. I respect the search.

Acknowledgements

Many people – too many to list – have contributed in some measure to the development of this book.

Especially we want to thank Catriona Grant, Rosie Kane, Peter Murray, and Eddie Truman, who have all provided valuable factual information; Felicity Garvie, for her painstaking organisational support; Kath Kyle, for taking on much of the responsibility for the production of the *Scottish Socialist Voice*, freeing Alan McCombes to work on this book.

Kevin Williamson, the commissioning editor of Rebel Inc, is one of Scotland's great pioneering publishers. His help and advice have been indispensable.

Finally, we would like to thank the many socialist activists in Scotland and further afield who have battled on valiantly to keep the flame alive, even during the tough times. Your courage has been an inspiration. Your time will come.

TS & AMcC

Introduction

by Tommy Sheridan

In a TV poll last year, viewers were asked to vote for the greatest song of the millennium. To my great delight, the winner was John Lennon's powerful and haunting song, 'Imagine'.

When he wrote 'Imagine', Lennon was going through an intensely political phase. He had marched against the Vietnam War, spoken out against global poverty, and donated money to the Upper Clyde Shipbuilders' work-in. The song itself evokes the vision of a socialist world, a world free from inequality, exploitation, racism, and war.

When we were racking our brains to come up with a title for this book, I suggested it be called *Imagine*. When the song was first released, I was still in my early years at primary school. Yet the ideals that inspired Lennon to write his celebrated song seem to me to have even greater resonance today than ever before.

The idea for this book first materialised towards the end of 1999. Soon after my election to the Scottish Parliament, I had undertaken a gruelling speaking tour of Scotland.

From draughty village halls in remote corners of the Highlands to fortified community centres in run-down city housing schemes, I had travelled thousands of miles and spoken to thousands of people. Socialism is supposed to be dead and buried with its ashes scattered to the four winds. Yet people were turning out in droves to these meetings, not to discuss some immediate pressing issue that affected their everyday lives, but to hear the general case for a socialist Scotland.

Even after 20 years of being bombarded from all sides with propaganda in support of the capitalist market economy, it is remarkable how many people remain attracted to the idea of building a new socialist society. Like John Lennon, they dream of something better.

Wherever I travelled, a few questions kept recurring. What exactly do you mean by socialism? In what ways would it be different from capitalism? Would a socialist Scotland be viable in a world economy run by giant multinational companies? And how do we go about changing society? Where do we start?

In a 30-minute speech, it's not possible to provide in-depth answers to these profound questions. It's only possible to scratch the surface. Yet many people are crying out for new ideas, for an alternative ideology. They look at the world they live in and they don't like what they see. They know what they are against; but they're not sure what they're for.

I discussed this with Alan McCombes, with whom I've worked closely over the years through numerous campaigns and political battles. We've laughed together, been locked up together, marched together, and been on hunger strike together. Alan is a man of action, but also a man of words. A talented socialist journalist, Alan became the founding editor in 1996 of the *Scottish Socialist Voice*, which is widely acclaimed as the best socialist newspaper on sale anywhere in Britain.

More than anyone, Alan has been at the cutting edge of developing and updating the ideas of socialism in Scotland, making them relevant to the 21st century. Working with him on this book was an education.

We bounced around a few ideas and eventually decided to write this book presenting the alternative to capitalism in a more in-depth way. We were clear that we didn't want to try to produce some academic treatise written for the benefit of economists or sociologists. Instead, we aimed to explain the case for an independent socialist Scotland and a global challenge to the rule of capitalism in language that ordinary people will understand.

The intention of this book is not just to argue the intellectual and moral case for socialism, but also to inspire people to get involved in the day-to-day fight to improve the lives of their families and communities.

In this book, we have tried to paint the big picture. But we also know that the struggle to transform society is a colossal project which will take years, perhaps decades, to accomplish. It won't be achieved in one big bang.

Socialism is about ideals and vision, but it is also about taking sides in the struggle against injustice and exploitation that is raging every day in workplaces and communities across Scotland and across the globe. Socialists are not just preachers seeking to convert people to the idea of a new form of society. We are also warriors fighting always on the side of the weak against the strong, on the side of the poor against the rich, on the side of the underdog against the powerful.

Sometimes it can seem that the odds are stacked hopelessly in favour of the rich and powerful, who have the legal, political, business, and media Establishment on their side. Yet, if we stand up for our beliefs with conviction and courage, we can win.

That's what the anti-Poll-Tax campaign showed. In the early days of that campaign, a whole procession of Labour politicans and leaders marched around Scotland, whipping up apathy and inciting defeatism. By contrast, ordinary people got themselves organised, took on the combined might of the Thatcher government, Labour-controlled councils, and the legal establishment, and brought the Poll Tax crashing down.

The reverberations of that victory are still resonating across

Scotland. In early 1992, I stood before three High Court judges for defying a court order to stop Scotland's first attempted Poll Tax warrant sale. I had never actually seen a warrant sale taking place.

But hatred of this medieval debt-recovery procedure is rooted in the folklore of working-class Scotland. My Gran, who lives in Govan, once told me a story of how a neighbour had returned from work to the sight of the contents of his home piled up outside his close. He ran upstairs, thinking that maybe there had been a fire. Instead he found his wife sobbing inconsolably. Their bits and pieces of chipped furniture stood on the pavement overnight, on display for everyone to see before the traders arrived to bid for them next morning.

For me, as for most people in Scotland, the Poll Tax itself was a disgrace, a barefaced attempt to transfer even more wealth from the poor to the rich. But the method now being used to recover Poll-Tax debts was even more inhuman. Two centuries ago, Scotland's national poet Robert Burns denounced the 18th-century forerunners of today's sheriff officers:

> 'They'll stamp and threaten, curse and swear,
> Apprehend you, poind your gear.'

I had been served with a court order banning me from the vicinity of the police headquarters in Turnbull Street in the East End of Glasgow, where the sale was scheduled to take place on October 1, 1991. But there are times when you have to make hard choices. My hatred of warrant sales far outweighed my fear of the legal consequences.

Along with 300 other anti-Poll-Tax activists, I marched into the courtyard where the sale was due to take place one hour later. I then tore up the interdict in full view of the TV cameras and called upon the assembled crowd to resist the warrant sale. And resist they did. The demonstrators surged forward towards the van, which contained the personal bits and pieces of a Greenock family. The massed ranks of blue uniforms were overwhelmed. The warrant sale was called off and, as the news was broadcast on local radio news bulletins, it seemed that the whole of Glasgow was cheering us to the rafters. 'VICTORY!' screamed the front-page banner headline in the Glasgow *Evening Times*.

A few months later, it was time to face the music. 'In a democratic society it is the rule of law that shields it from anarchy and mob rule . . . many forms of political protest are available but ignoring court orders and obstructing sheriff officers are not among their number,' proclaimed Lord Caplan, pomposity oozing from every pore as he delivered the sentence – six months' imprisonment.

Eight years later I stood on Edinburgh's Royal Mile, just a few hundred yards from the courtroom from which I had been led handcuffed, bound for Saughton Prison. But I was now an elected MSP, and I'm proud to say that I achieved that position without compromising or diluting a single principle.

Once again, I was surrounded by photographers, journalists, and TV crews. But this time round, I was being treated like a hero rather than a villain. The Bill I had introduced to outlaw warrant sales and poindings had just provoked the first full-scale mutiny in the year-old Scottish Parliament and was now on course to become law.

Just as I had been singled out for special punishment years before, I was now being singled out for special praise. I deserved neither. The defeat of Scotland's first attempted warrant sale at Turnbull Street had been a glorious victory. It was a turning point in the battle to make the Tory Poll Tax uncollectable. But there were 300 people there that day, and every one of them played a heroic role in stopping that attempted warrant sale from going ahead.

As a Scottish Socialist MSP I initiated the Bill to abolish warrant sales and poindings. But I had received crucial backing from fellow MSPs, John McAllion and Alex Neil. I had been provided with indispensable expert guidance from solicitor Mike Dailly. Voluntary organisations, too, had thrown their weight behind the Bill. The Scottish Socialist Party had mobilised public support for the Bill up and down Scotland. And, before the Scottish Socialist Party was even formed, the Scottish Anti-Poll Tax Federation had fought the sheriff officers to a standstill in a guerrilla war without bullets which had raged across Scotland for the best part of a decade.

The removal of this centuries-old piece of repressive legislation was not a personal victory for one individual; it was a collective victory fought and won by thousands of ordinary people after a decade of struggle.

There are two powerful lessons that I believe should be learned from our successful struggle to end the shameful practice of warrant sales and poindings. The first is that we should never assume that just because some people have money, or status, or power, or titles, or even wigs and gowns, that they are right and we are wrong.

The other lesson is that the battle against injustice has to be waged on all fronts. The mainstream political parties are fixated with elected posts. Some politicians may occasionally participate in this or that demonstration. But everything is subordinated to the winning of positions in government. Elections, parliaments, councils, are the be-all and end-all and everything else is a distraction.

Some politicians act with the best of intentions, others with the worst of intentions. But most are united in their aim of grabbing power and running things from on high while the lower orders look on in admiration. 'Leave politics to the politicians' is the unspoken message that they convey.

There are a growing number of people who are now reacting in the opposite direction. Many of the young people protesting on the streets of Seattle, Washington, and London against global capitalism reject politics out of hand. They are so filled with contempt for the politicians that they deny the legitimacy of any elections, any parliaments, any form of organised politics.

I can understand where they are coming from. They are justified in treating politicians and political parties with suspicion. The American tycoon, Henry Ford, who pioneered mass production of motor cars, had a favourite catchphrase: 'You can have any colour of car you like,' he said, 'as long as it's black!' These days, cars come in all colours, shapes and sizes. But our politicians tend to come in one colour – monochrome grey. In the four big political parties, the grey men in the grey suits hold sway at every level.

Young people are right to take to the streets. Some of these protests have occasionally got out of hand, providing an excuse for sleek politicians to appear on TV to denounce the 'anarchy and disorder'. Personally, I would rather young people were out protesting against capitalism than shooting heroin into their veins in a back alley, or carving each other up with broken bottles after a Saturday night on the booze. But what the Establishment fears more than anything else is the fusion of direct action with political struggle to win over the hearts and minds of the majority of the population.

The battle to transform society will only be victorious with the active involvement of millions of ordinary people. We won't change society simply by convincing people to vote for us; although that's part of it, because if we can't convince people to *vote* for change, neither will we be able to convince them to *struggle* for change.

This book is about trying to raise people's sights beyond the humdrum day-to-day concerns that all of us have. It is a call to everyone in Scotland to look beyond the gloss and the hype of modern capitalism and to consider the possibility that things could be different.

The great black American civil-rights campaigner, Martin Luther King, once offered up his dream of the future: 'Some day children will learn words whose meanings they do not understand. Children in India will ask, "What is hunger?" Children in Hiroshima will ask, "What is an atomic bomb?" Children in Alabama will ask, "What is segregation?" And we will say to them, "These are words that no longer have meaning, so we have removed them from the dictionary."'

Is it too far-fetched to dream that one day children growing up in Scotland will ask, 'What was poverty? What was deprivation? What was homelessness?' Or that children growing up in Central Europe will ask, 'What was ethnic cleansing? What was torture? What was war?' Or that children all over the world will ask, 'What was famine? What was inequality? What was exploitation?'

Part One

GIVE ME SOME TRUTH

I'm sick and tired of hearing things
From uptight short-sighted narrow-minded hypocrites
All I want is the truth
Just gimme some truth now.

Chapter One

FROM EASTERHOUSE TO ETHIOPIA

IT'S THE FINAL Christmas of the 20th century, and across the world, people are preparing to celebrate the dawn of a new millennium.

In a small town in Central Scotland, an elderly couple shiver in the cold and dark. Mary has left her pension book in a neighbour's home but, like many women of her generation, is too proud to ask for help. She's managed to scrape together £5 to buy a power card, but because the couple have used up their £14 emergency credit, it's not enough to restore the electricity supply.

A few days later, the body of her husband, Willie, is removed from their home. A retired miner who has spent most of his working life toiling away underground to provide society with heat and light, Willie has frozen to death.[1]

While he lies lifeless in his bed, Strathclyde Police are holding a press conference 30 miles away to announce the 146th drugs-related death in the region since the start of the year. If that number of young people perished in a plane crash or a fire in a nightclub, the whole nation would have been in mourning for weeks on end. But most of these young people are heroin addicts, mainlining the drug into their veins in the back streets of some of Europe's bleakest, most impoverished housing estates. The director of the government-sponsored drugs campaign, Scotland Against Drugs, tells the press conference, 'One thing that strikes you when you speak to many young drug users is that people often don't care whether they live or die.'[2]

These two incidents span a 50-year generation gap. At one end are thousands of men and women who have spent their lives toiling away in pits, factories, docks, and shipyards, who have raised families, who have fought in wars. Now they live out their final days scraping together enough cash for a power card to heat their homes.

At the other end are thousands of young people who have never worked because they were born at the wrong time, in the wrong housing scheme, in the wrong city. They have no present and no future, so they destroy their bodies and brains with lethal concoctions supplied by criminal drugs gangs.

Scotland is by no stretch of the imagination a Third World country. The land where pensioners freeze to death in their homes is a land teeming with natural and man-made energy, including oil, gas, electricity, coal, hydro and nuclear power. The city where young people die on the streets every couple of days is a 50-minute train journey from one of the richest financial centres in Europe, whose banks control funds worth £300 billion, or £60,000 for every man, woman, and child in Scotland.[3]

A generation ago, Gunther Stent, the pioneer of microbiology, wrote a book which was hailed as a visionary insight into the bright brand-new world that lay ahead. Published in 1969, *The Coming of the Golden Age: A View of the End of Progress* anticipated the end of poverty, starvation, disease and war.[4]

Within a generation or so, according to Stent, science would solve all of the pressing problems of society. Gradually, the Third World would prosper, eventually catching up with Europe and North America. Meanwhile social inequality within the more advanced countries would diminish as living standards were 'levelled up'. Worldwide economic progress would in turn reduce national and ethnic antagonisms, consigning warfare to the toxic waste dump of history. Even pollution would be eradicated as new techniques were developed for harnessing energy.

By all the laws of logic, Stent's predictions should have been fulfilled by now. Back in 1969, when *The Golden Age* was published, the technical means and the resources already existed to feed, clothe and house every human being comfortably. Since then, technological progress has accelerated at a dizzying pace. We can send spaceships to the far-flung reaches of our solar system to photograph distant planets. Microcomputers that can fit into the palm of the hand can transmit whole libraries of information instantaneously across the globe. We have learned to perform medical miracles, including heart, lung, and liver transplants. We have begun to unravel the mysteries of human DNA, and even to clone animals.

Yet, to paraphrase the French proverb, the more things have changed, the more they have remained the same. Poverty, starvation, disease, pollution, racism, and war continue to stalk the planet. If anything, whole tracts of the Third World are even more impoverished today than they were 30 years ago.

Back in 1973, the President of the World Bank, Robert McNamara, addressed the annual conference of that organisation and declared, 'We should strive to eradicate poverty by end of the century.'[5]

Today the World Bank confesses that 1.2 billion live in 'extreme poverty', with a total income of less than 66 pence a day. It calculates that three billion people – half the world's population – survives on less than £1 a day. The organisation also admits that the poorest 63 countries, containing 57 per cent of the earth's population, receive just six per cent of all income.[6]

And the gap between rich and poor is growing wider every day, both within countries and between countries. A United Nations report published at the start of the 21st century makes the point that global inequalities increased in the course of the 20th century by 'a magnitude out of proportion to anything ever experienced before'. The lifespan in the poorest African countries is now half that of the richest countries. The report explains that, in 1820, the gap between the richest and poorest countries was three to one. By 1950 it had risen to 35 to one. Today it is 74 to one.[7]

Back in 1984, the Ethiopian famine aroused the sympathy of the whole planet. Huge charity extravaganzas, including Band Aid, were staged to help alleviate the suffering. The spotlight was turned full glare on Third World starvation and governments across the world came under pressure to ensure such a calamity could never again occur.

More than 15 years later, the charity Christian Aid estimates that in the continent of Africa a child dies prematurely every five seconds. Some starve to death because their families are too poor to buy food. Others die of 'preventable' diseases, because their governments cannot afford to buy medicines.

In this glittering new hi-tech global economy of the 21st century, one in three children in the world are malnourished. Another 250 million child labourers under the age of 14 toil away in Third World factories and farms. Millions more are sold into slavery or prostitution. Others have their limbs amputated to attract more money when they are sent out to beg on the streets. Many have their organs removed and sold for transplants.

As this social catastrophe spreads and multiplies, charities battle on in a valiant attempt to relieve the suffering. Every year, high-profile events such as Comic Relief bring scenes of total destitution to our TV screens. In 1999, the event announced a record-breaking £27.4 million raised, which is a tribute to the generosity of ordinary people the length and breadth of the UK. But, compared to the real wealth that is swilling around the planet, £27 million is like a grain of sand in the desert. Every single day, 25,000 times that sum – £750 billion – is gambled away on the world's stock exchanges and currency markets.[8]

In contrast to the mass destitution that blights the southern hemisphere, the prosperous north produces and consumes more material wealth than ever before. Fifteen per cent of the world's population – mainly in Europe, North America, and Japan – receives nearly 80 per cent of the planet's income, according to the World Bank.[9] Millions of families now have access to cars, TVs, telephones, videos, central heating, microwave ovens, fridge-freezers and dishwashers. We live in an affluent society. In the words of George Kerevan, the guru of the Thatcherite wing of Scottish nationalism, 'These days we all shop at Gap and drink designer beer.'[10] At least, that's what we're told. But is it true?

It is certainly true that there are plenty of people who buy fashionable clothes and relax at the weekend over a couple of beers. But, then again, most of these people work long hours and produce fat profits for their employers. There are also plenty of people who buy their clothes at Poundstretchers or What Everyone Wants rather than Gap. And there are others, usually seen huddled in shop doorways in our city centres, who don't shop anywhere, drink anywhere or, for that matter, live anywhere.

At the same time, there are people who will cheerfully pay £2000 for a bottle of wine in Edinburgh's more exclusive restaurants – a year's income for an unemployed single person – and others who will splash out ten times that sum on a new party dress.

It's true that there are less mega-rich people in Scotland than there are in Los Angeles or London. It's also true that far fewer people in Scotland are destitute than in Lima or Lagos. But, far from being a classless nation, modern-day Caledonia is a grotesquely divided society where elements of Beverly Hills meet elements of the Third World.

An exaggeration? Not according to the Malnutrition Advisory Group. In early 2000, the organisation produced a shock report revealing that half of all patients admitted to hospital in Scotland's biggest city, Glasgow, are suffering from malnutrition. The advisory group estimates that 65,000 people in the city, one in ten of the total population, are so undernourished that they are vulnerable to disease.[11]

Other surveys have shown that 43 per cent of pupils attending primary and secondary schools in the city receive free school meals, while 58 per cent are eligible for clothing and footwear grants because their parents cannot afford to buy these items.[12]

At a seminar for Members of the Scottish Parliament in August 1999, social policy expert Professor David Donnison produced figures showing that, across Scotland as a whole, 25 per cent of the population – 1.2 million people – live in households which are officially designated as poor. Most of these households include young children: 34 per cent of all Scottish children, and 41 per cent of under-fives, live on or below the poverty line. 'People do not recognise the gravity of the crisis we face,' Professor Donnison told the seminar.

Some people would like to pretend that poverty does not exist in this country: 'But these people are not really poor. They live in the lap of luxury compared to the starving millions in Africa. Real poverty might have existed in Britain in the 1930s, but not nowadays.'

Usually the people who make such claims live in nice suburban homes, send their children to expensive private schools, and have small fortunes – or sometimes even large fortunes – stashed away in stocks, shares, and investment accounts.

No-one would seriously claim that poverty in Glasgow or Liverpool today is directly comparable with starvation in Ethiopia or Mozambique. But poverty is not a straightforward financial equation.

A few years ago, community worker Mari Marcel Thekaekara came to Scotland from India with her husband. Their intention was to reverse the stereotype of an aid worker from a wealthy country travelling to the other side of the world to help the poor.

She described her experiences to the *New Internationalist* magazine: 'We were told that the Easterhouse housing estate in Glasgow was considered Europe's worst slum. We thought this was ludicrous. These people had assured housing, electricity, hot and cold water, refrigerators, and cookers. By Indian standards this was middle-class luxury.

'But then it hit us. Most of the men in Easterhouse hadn't had a job in 20 years. They were dispirited and depressed, often alcoholic. Emotionally and mentally, they were far worse off than the poor where we lived, even though the physical trappings of poverty were less stark.

'The Easterhouse men who'd been jobless for 20 years felt far more hopeless than people in India who scrabbled in garbage heaps to feed their kids, though both groups were at the bottom of society.'[13]

Many older people who grew up during the Great Depression of the 1930s will claim that 'we were poor, but we were happy'. Of course, people's memories can play tricks with the passage of time. Often, it's the good experiences that you remember and the bad experiences that you repress.

People weren't exactly dancing in the streets when unemployment in Glasgow reached 50 per cent in the mid-1930s. Instead there was an outpouring of rage, expressed in hunger marches and in the growth of radical political parties.

Across Europe, fascism, which fed on mass unemployment and destitution, came from nowhere to conquer power in one country after another. At the opposite end of the political spectrum, communist parties and other left-wing organisations mushroomed into mass movements.

Yet there is more than a grain of truth in the rose-tinted reminiscences of some older people as they recall the sense of community and solidarity that made life more tolerable even in the darkest days of the Hungry Thirties.

In those days, everyone was in the same boat. Material deprivation was accepted as a normal part of working-class existence. The communitarian culture and extended families of the tenements and pit villages provided a rudimentary form of local socialism in which everyone looked out for everyone else.

That is not to romanticise the past. People nowadays have greater freedom to choose where they live, how they live, and who they live with. There is greater tolerance of diversity. But, as the old structures and institutions break down, people are becoming more isolated, more pessimistic, more fearful of the future, more ground down by the stresses and strains of everyday life. A recent survey by the Lloyds TSB Life Index found that in Scotland only 41 per cent of the population are optimistic about the future. According to the Royal Society of Medicine, depression has reached epidemic proportions worldwide and costs the UK economy £2 billion a year.[14]

Day in, day out, we are bombarded with images of glamour, wealth, and success. Back in the mid-1960s Mick Jagger lampooned the advertising industry in the classic Rolling Stones song, 'Satisfaction'.

> 'And that man comes on to tell me
> just how white my shirts should be.
> But he can't be a man 'cos he doesn't
> smoke the same cigarettes as me.'

Yet, back then, advertising was a gentle amateur affair compared with the manic multi-billion-pound marketing industry of the 21st century. Huge psychological pressures bear down, especially on those at the bottom of society, to wear the right clothes, drink the right beer, drive the right car, sport the right trainers, wear the right perfume or aftershave, buy the right toys for their children.

But as everyone knows, outward appearances can be deceptive. Many of the same people who sport designer labels live in dilapidated housing, exist on poor diets, suffer ill health – and are up to their ears in debt.

Poverty is not just a matter of inconvenience to those who suffer it; it's a matter of life and death. On average, a male Glaswegian will die six years younger than the average Englishman. A female Glaswegian will die five years younger than her English counterpart. Glaswegians in general are twice as likely to die before the age of 65 than their affluent neighbours just across the city boundary in Bearsden.[15]

At the start of a new century, despair weighs down like a gravestone in the hearts of hundreds of thousands of Scots. In an eloquent expression of this sense of hopelessness, a tenants' leader in Glasgow's run-down Possil housing scheme told the *Scottish Socialist Voice*, 'The flats here are damp, the curtains meet in the middle of the room because of the draughts, and every second kid has an asthma inhaler. This is the Third World. Some people call it Bangladesh.'[16]

Chapter Two

WHO NEEDS CLASS WAR, ANYWAY?

MILLIONS OF PEOPLE across the UK dream of winning the jackpot on the National Lottery and becoming overnight millionaires. The chances are that if you keep buying a ticket every Wednesday and Saturday you will eventually hit the jackpot. That's on one condition – that you live for about 20,000 years.

Just imagine, then, waking up in the morning to discover you're £2 million richer than you were yesterday. The following morning you're another £2 million richer. Every day you wake up, you've won another lottery jackpot. Within a month you're a millionaire 60 times over. And by the end of a year, your personal wealth has increased by £740 million.

For 20 people in Britain today, this is no idle fantasy. During 1999, 20 individuals, including the Duke of Westminster, Richard Branson, and the shadowy Barclay twins, who own the *Scotsman* newspaper, saw their wealth rise on average by £2 million a day.[1]

On a global scale, the wealth that is now concentrated in the hands of the ultra-rich is even more fantastic. If the richest man on the planet, Bill Gates, was a country, he would rank 38th richest nation in the world out of 200. At the start of the millennium, his personal wealth was calculated at £50 billion, a sum of money which no individual could ever hope to spend. If he went on the most extravagant spending spree imaginable, lashing out £1 million every day, it would take the Microsoft boss 136 years to spend his fortune.

In a *Newsnight* interview with Gates, presenter Jeremy Paxman made the point that if he were to drop a $10,000 bill on the floor, it would not be worthwhile for the computer tycoon to reach down and pick it up – because in the time it took him to do that, he'd be more than $10,000 richer anyway.[2]

When the tomb of Tutankhamen was excavated in 1922, it was discovered to contain a dazzling collection of works of art and a solid gold coffin. But the extravagant lifestyles led by the ultra-rich of the 21st century make the Pharaohs of ancient Egypt look like Spartans by comparison.

Imagine a mansion made entirely of gold. The floors and ceilings are gold. The tables and furniture are gold. The doors and walls are gold. The cutlery and crockery are gold. This is not a fantasy Hollywood film set, but a real house in the United States.

Then there's the watch that's locked away in a bank vault in Geneva. Encrusted with 118 emerald-cut diamonds, it's known as the Kalista, after the Greek word which means 'most magnificent'. And magnificent it certainly should be, because it's currently valued at £6 million. Or at least that was its value at the start of the year 2000, but every day the value of the Kalista watch appreciates by a further £25,000.

These are perhaps extreme examples of ostentatious luxury. More everyday transactions include the bottles of Pinot Noir that sell for £10,000 each in top restaurants, the Rolls-Royce cars that sell for £150,000, the Gulfstream private jets that cost £50 million, the private yachts that cost £5 million, the £10,000 Hermès handbags, the baby grand pianos which sell for £100,000, the racehorses, the helicopters, the art treasures, the private gymnasiums, the private spas and whirlpools.

A truly incredible amount of human labour and natural resources are devoted to furnishing a tiny minority of the world's population with every luxury imaginable, and some which are unimaginable. A Rolls-Royce for example, takes six months to construct. Every engine is completely hand-built. The interior includes hand-finished leather hides, precisely fitted luxury carpets, and exquisitely hand-crafted walnut wood panelling. A small army of highly skilled electricians, engineers, mechanics, upholsterers, painters, and carpenters spend half a year assembling a single vehicle that will then become the exclusive personal property of a single individual.

Yet the work involved in assembling a Rolls-Royce is negligible compared to the time, labour and materials that go into the construction of a luxury yacht, for example, or a private helicopter. It is truly amazing that this gargantuan devouring of resources by the ultra-rich is taken for granted while health spending in Africa — a continent plagued by some of the most dreadful diseases known to science — works out at a miserable £4.50 per person per year.[3]

According to most mainstream politicians, businessmen, and media commentators, the co-existence of rich and poor is as natural and inevitable as the co-existence of the sun and the rain. The rich are rich because they deserve to be rich. They are more talented, more hardworking, more dynamic, and more intelligent than the rest of us. And in any case, the wealth they accumulate trickles down to the very depths of society, so we all benefit. Indeed, the more the rich get richer, the more the poor get richer.

That's what we're told, anyway — and you'd better believe it, because it's not just the Tories who worship before the 'creators of wealth' and insist that, without them, all of civilisation would grind to a halt. One New Labour Minister, Stephen Byers, told the big-business CBI conference in 1999, 'Wealth creation is more important than wealth redistribution.'

His boss, Tony Blair, insists, 'Britain needs more successful people who can become rich.' He repeatedly assures us, 'The class war is over.'[4]

For the 5000 people in Britain who earned over £500,000 last year, that is good news indeed. Who needs class war when you're busy maintaining a smattering of stately homes, chic apartments, and Mediterranean villas? Why fritter away your precious time on old-fashioned pursuits like class warfare when you can be lounging around the golf course, skiing in the Rocky Mountains or sunning yourself in the Seychelles?

The truth is, the rich may not preach class war so much these days, but they practise it ceaselessly. Every week in British industry and commerce, top executives are awarded special bonuses for increasing profits and share prices. As a general rule, they achieve these results by sacking workers, cutting wages, worsening conditions, and coercing their workforces into working a little bit harder. In other words, the rich get richer, not by trickling wealth down to the working class and the poor, but by making the working class and the poor even poorer.

The statistics for the growth of wealth and poverty in Britain over the past 20 years strip bare the myth of the so-called 'trickle-down theory'. Far from trickling down from the rich to the poor, wealth has trickled upwards – or, more accurately, cascaded upwards – from the poor to the rich. In 1979, five million people in Britain lived below the poverty line. Today – even though we are told that the economy has never been in better shape – there are 14 million people living in poverty.[5]

Meanwhile, the rich grow richer . . . and richer . . . and richer. Today, according to the latest *Sunday Times* Rich List, just 1000 individuals – 0.002 per cent of the UK population – have a combined personal wealth totalling £180 billion. Such a sum of money is almost incomprehensible to mere mortals. It is more than ten times greater than the entire annual budget that the

Scottish Parliament has to spend on health, education, housing, local government, emergency services, social services, and everything else it is responsible for. It is triple the Gross Domestic Product (ie the total amount of wealth, goods and services produced) of Nigeria, with over 100 million inhabitants.[6]

Speaking at a conference of the Women's Institute in the year 2000, the New Labour Prime Minister assured the assembled gathering that he no longer believes in 'egalitarianism that levels people down'. Tony Blair's claim to have once believed in egalitarianism is perhaps open to dispute. But there's no disputing his claim that he now rejects any notions of social equality. In the 12 months preceding his speech to the Women's Institute, the wealth of Britain's richest 1000 people had grown by an astronomical £27 billion under a New Labour government, beating all previous records hands down.

It is true that some of the wealth of the rich does percolate down to other layers of society. In the City of London, Porsche and Ferrari dealers, cocaine dealers, champagne importers, and people who own high-class restaurants, exclusive fashion labels, and expensive jewellery shops are just some of the people who have benefited from the booming stock exchange.

But that's about as far as the wealth of the City trickles. It doesn't even trickle down the Thames as far as Bethnal Green or Tower Hamlets. In these areas, the 'People of the Abyss', as they were described by socialist writer Jack London at the beginning of last century, can still be seen, huddled under railway arches or bringing up children in damp, vermin-infested tenements.

Nor does the claim that the rich deserve more money because of their special talents stand up to serious scrutiny. Some people are more talented than others, there's no argument about that. But the main talent possessed by most of Britain's hyper-rich is a talent for being born into the right family.

We are repeatedly told that the old rigid lines of division

between the classes have been erased from society. In Tony Blair's Cool Britannia, we are informed, the old aristocracy is a dying breed. The class that once ruled over five continents is now forced to take to the streets in the type of protest demos traditionally associated with the working class for the right to gallop through the countryside in red coats and top hats shouting, 'Tally ho!'

Times are changing and inherited wealth is on its way out, usurped by entrepreneurs who have clawed their way up the financial ladder by talent and sheer hard work. If they can do it, you can do it. That's what we're asked to believe – but is it true?

Every year for the past 12 years, the *Sunday Times* magazine has produced a league table of the richest people in Britain, with a potted biography of these individuals. The magazine confesses that it tends to be cautious in its estimates, because so much of the wealth of the rich is hidden away beneath a complex labyrinth of secret bank accounts, fictitious trust funds, and overseas investments. Even so, these understated figures reveal that the wealth of the mega-rich in Britain approximately tripled between 1995 and 2000.

It also shows that, contrary to Nouveau Labour mythology, most of them definitely don't start out as bus drivers or stallholders at the Barras. Of the 50 richest people in Scotland, more than half inherited their businesses and property.[7] Some of that property can be traced back to the early Middle Ages, when the ancestors of today's landowners marauded around the countryside looting and pillaging, like medieval versions of today's gangland drug barons. Others took over businesses initially set up by their parents or grandparents.

Instead of tending to diminish over time, the trend towards inherited wealth intensifies as wealth becomes more and more concentrated in fewer and fewer hands. As the rich accumulate more and more wealth, the less of it they are able to spend themselves, and the more is left over to pass down to their descendants.

Nor is it true that the super-rich are mainly made up these days of talented footballers, pop stars, and other entertainers. Only two entertainers, Paul McCartney and Andrew Lloyd-Webber, and no sports stars make it into Britain's top 100.[8]

Further down the list is DJ Chris Evans, estimated to be worth over £100 million. He at least has the good grace to be embarrassed about his income. 'When you've got this much money, you can't spend it all. Obscene is definitely the word for it,' he points out.

Most of the 'self-made rich' don't have any special talents, except perhaps for gambling. Although the public spotlight tends to focus on entrepreneurs such as Bill Gates or Stagecoach boss Brian Souter, most serious wealth is created not by investing in industry, transport, or communications, but by gambling on the stock exchanges, the property markets, and the currency markets. London-based billionaire George Soros, for example, once made £1 billion in a single week, betting against the pound on the international currency markets.

Of the 5000 people in the UK who earned over £500,000 last year, more than three quarters work in 'financial services'.[9] That means they buy and sell shares, or they buy and sell currency, or they buy and sell currency or shares for other people, or they advise people which shares or currency to buy and sell. One thing they don't do is produce anything of value, or provide any useful service to society. They simply shift money around.

At least the old 'Captains of Industry' were able to claim they built ships, or produced coal, or manufactured cars, or turned iron into steel. Of course, they did none of these things. They employed other people to build ships, dig coal, manufacture cars, and turn iron into steel, while they sat in boardroom meetings discussing balance sheets. That's when they weren't footering around on the golf course or sunning themselves on Mediterranean beaches. But today's Great British financial entrepreneurs can't even make the fictitious claim that they are useful.

Whenever firefighters, train drivers, miners, nurses, lorry drivers, cleansing workers, power workers, water workers, teachers, ambulance drivers, threaten industrial action, panic invariably sweeps through the corridors of power. Newspaper editors are mobilised to whip up hysteria against the discontented group of workers. Police are dispatched to the picket lines. Sometimes a state of emergency is even declared and the army put on standby.

But let's imagine Britain's property speculators, for example, were to go on strike. How on earth could the NHS possibly function? How could the transport system operate? How could the power grid continue to supply energy? Surely the army would have to be called in to take over the functions of these financial wizards?

The truth is that society would carry on functioning as normal. Even if the rich were to mount an all-out indefinite general strike involving every stockbroker, shareholder, investment analyst, fund manager, currency trader, property speculator, and company director, most of us would scarcely even notice the difference.

In the days of Queen Victoria, churchmen, industrialists, and politicians liked to pontificate about 'the deserving poor' and 'the undeserving poor'. What we have today is a bloated upper class which could accurately be described as 'the undeserving rich'. It constitutes a tiny fraction of society, yet it siphons off a huge chunk of wealth. Far from being indispensable, the average member of this exclusive club is about as about as useful and necessary as a gallstone in the bladder.

Chapter Three

THE AGE OF RAGE

TIM STONE WAS once a brilliant scientist specialising in lung diseases. He earned a comfortable salary, lived in a luxury mansion with his wife and children and was so renowned in his field that he was even listed in the *Who's Who in the World* next to Sharon Stone, the film actress. When Scotland's Education Minister, Sam Galbraith, fell seriously ill after contracting a rare lung disease, Tim Stone helped find a cure.

But then, all of a sudden, Tim's world was turned upside down. The Freeman Hospital in Newcastle, where he worked, told him his services were no longer required. After being made redundant, he was unable to find another job. The type of work he did was highly specialised, performed by just 12 people in the whole of the UK.

His life began to fall apart. He hit the bottle and soon became an alcoholic. His marriage collapsed. He ran up huge debts and lost his home. His health deteriorated and he was diagnosed with mouth cancer. Towards the end of 1999, he was found dead after falling from a balcony. There was a suggestion that he had been fleeing from people from whom he had borrowed money.

At the inquest into his death, Tim's step-daughter blamed the NHS for his death. 'We are certain of one thing,' she said. 'None of this would have happened if he had not lost his job.'[1]

Most economists and politicians would confess that there is inequality at the two opposite extremes of wealth and poverty.

But the rest of us are supposed to have become comfortably incorporated into the middle classes. Some sociologists talk of the 'diamond-shaped society' – with a small ultra-rich 'overclass' at the top, a small impoverished 'underclass' at the bottom, and a big wide swathe in the middle.

They point to the changed make-up of the workforce in Scotland and other developed countries as evidence to support this proposition. It's certainly true that there have been big changes over the past couple of decades. For example, in the 1950s there were over 100,000 coal miners in Scotland. Now they have become almost an extinct species, as central to our modern economy as barber's pole painters, chimney sweeps and bookies' runners.

On Clydeside, there were once 100,000 shipyard workers; today there are more people making a living from selling illegal drugs than from building ships. Call centres and fast-food outlets have begun to replace the engineering factories and steelworks that once formed the bedrock of the Scottish economy. Across Britain as a whole, more people work in Indian restaurants than in coal mining, steel manufacturing and shipbuilding combined.

But the working class is not just made up of shipyard workers, coal miners, mill workers, car assembly workers, bricklayers and such-like. It is a much broader social formation, involving a vast assortment of people with diverse lifestyles and working conditions. It includes more or less everyone who works for an employer, from fast-food sellers to fashion models, from orchestral musicians to office cleaners, from computer programmers to college lecturers.

Contrary to the mythology that we are fed by politicians and sociologists, the working class is not vanishing; nor is the middle class growing. In fact, the trend is moving in exactly the opposite direction. As the example of Tim Stone illustrates, the solid middle ground of society is gradually turning to quicksand.

In the past, big sections of the unskilled manual working class lived a precarious existence. Dockers, for example, used to queue up at the quayside whenever a ship arrived in port, hoping desperately to be chosen for a few days' work by the foreman. Building workers have always drifted from job to job, and often from city to city, in search of short-term work.

But, especially from the Second World War onwards, the vast majority of workers began to enjoy a reasonably stable and secure lifestyle with a regular wage, paid holidays and paid sick leave. Many people would start work at 15 and retire 50 years later from the same firm. Even those who were made redundant could at least expect a sizeable lump-sum payment, to tide them over until they found another job.

But times are changing rapidly. 'You can't expect a job for life,' we are now told, often by wealthy businessmen who inherit their businesses from their parents and will in turn hand their businesses down to their children. A whole new business vocabulary has been constructed, including terms such as 'the flexible labour market', 'casualisation', 'deregulation', 'contracting out', 'competitive tendering', 'downsizing', 'performance-related pay', 'outsourcing'. Just as the Eskimoes have 100 words for snow, the corporate slavedrivers of the 21st century have 100 different euphemisms for exploitation.

In his book, *False Dawn: Delusions of Global Capitalism* Professor John Gray of the London School of Economics points out: 'For much of the population, traditional bourgeois institutions such as career structures and vocations no longer exist. The result is a re-proletarianisation of much of the industrial working class and the debourgeoisification of what remains of the former middle classes.' Or, to put it in more everyday language, the working class is becoming more and more working class … and the middle class is becoming less and less middle class.

According to the 1999 survey of British Social Attitudes, 60 per cent of workers in the UK are unhappy in their jobs. They report feelings of exhaustion, stress, and insecurity. Psychologists warn of the intensifying pressure and strain which are taking their toll on the physical and mental health of millions.

No-one can dispute the fact that material living standards, particularly for skilled and professional workers, have improved over the past decade or so. There are higher levels of home ownership and car ownership than ever before. A whole new range of consumer goods, such as videos, dishwashers, microwave ovens and personal computers, have become widely available in recent years.

But these modest gains disguise the fact that the working class is being exploited more ruthlessly and systematically than ever before. American economist John Schmitt points out that the average American worker produces 12 per cent more in the course of an hour's work than ten years ago.[2] Yet, allowing for inflation, wages have increased by less than two per cent.

Meanwhile, a report by the banking company Merrill Lynch admits that the minimum wage in the US has fallen by 20 per cent in real terms over the past 20 years.[3] The general trend across all the developed countries has been more or less the same. In Spain, the economy doubled in size over 20 years; yet the numbers in employment fell by eight per cent. Right across the globe, people are working harder and longer for less pay and in worsening conditions.

This is a startling turnaround. In the past, even when times were tough, people looked forward to the future with confidence. 'Things Can Only Get Better' was New Labour's cynical theme tune during the 1997 general election. But for generation after generation throughout the 20th century, that really was the prevailing belief.

There was a feeling among all classes in society – at least in developed countries such as Britain and the US – that tomorrow would be better than today, that next year would be better than this year, that the next generation would have a better life than this generation.

That sense of optimism was well grounded. One American economist, Robert Lawrence, has calculated that, from 1870 until 1970, living standards doubled every 35 years. Each generation was approximately twice as well off as the preceding generation.[4]

In Britain, there was a similar sense of eternal progress, especially in the post-war years. The NHS was founded, making free health care available to everyone for the first time in history. The welfare state was established, providing a safety net to ensure that no-one would starve. Huge resources were ploughed into education. Slums were torn down and replaced with gleaming new housing schemes with baths and inside toilets. Unemployment seemed to have been banished forever, and the Great Depression of the 1930s became a distant folk memory. 'You've never had it so good,' said Tory Prime Minister, Harold Macmillan, with some justification.

Now people look to the future with foreboding. They live in houses that they can't really afford. They drive cars that they can't really afford. They buy clothes and household goods that they can't really afford. They work incredibly long hours and pile up terrifyingly large debts in order to live the lifestyle they are told they must have.

And, notwithstanding the cheerful twitterings of most politicians, there is a growing body of opinion that insists that things can only get worse.

A number of sociologists and economists warn of the mass elimination of tens of millions of jobs across the developed countries as a result of automation. Jeremy Rifkin, President of the Washington DC-based Foundation on Economic Trends, who has written extensively on the impact of new technology on the workforce, maintains that 'the shift from mass to elite labour forces is what distinguishes work in the Information Age from work in the Industrial Age'.

Predicting the disappearance of scores of occupations, including assembly-line work, clerical work, bank telling, telephone operating, and many others, Rifkin warns 'With near workerless factories and virtual companies already looming on the horizon, every nation will have to grapple with the question of what to do with the millions of people whose labour is needed less, or not at all.'[5]

More brutally, Professor Ian Angell of the London School of Economics, who provides advice to some of the world's biggest multinational corporations on future trends in society, sketches out a chilling vision of a new Frankenstein capitalism, where the advance of technology, instead of liberating the human race, causes the virtual collapse of civilisation. 'The lights are going out for wide sectors of society and for whole categories of employment. We are entering a new Dark Age: an age of hopelessness, an Age of Rage.'

The Professor insists that a new industrial revolution has begun which will leave most of the population surplus to requirements as a new intellectual, business, and cultural elite rises to the top. 'Mass production methods needed an over-supply of humanity – now there is a glut,' he says, quite matter-of-factly. He goes on, 'A large population, particularly an uneducated and ageing population, has now become the major problem.'

Not that Professor Angell loses too much sleep over the fate of those whom he decries as 'society's losers'. He describes taxation of business as 'state-sponsored extortion'. He lauds the fact that the rich are getting richer and the poor poorer, and says that 'the call for fairness is the mere whingeing of failures and parasites.'

Alarmingly, Professor Angell insists, 'The biggest challenge of the coming decades is how to find an acceptable means to scale back democracy.' This is taboo territory for most politicians, so the man should at least be commended for his honesty. Indeed, it's clear that the arrogant professor is simply blurting out publicly ideas which many global political and business leaders privately adhere to.

Fortunately, Professor Angell's analysis of the impact of technology on society is one-sided, leading him to paint an exaggeratedly apocalyptic picture. For example, he states that 'The Marxist myth that labour creates wealth will be buried once and for all . . . it is that rare commodity, human intellect, which is the stuff of tomorrow's world.'[6]

It is a delusion to imagine that even in the new Information Age, businessmen, intellectuals, and machines can supplant the traditional working class as the backbone of the economy and society. It's true that electronic communications and the development of high-speed data-processing techniques have boosted productivity and have increased all-round efficiency. This, along with the driving down of labour costs through deregulation and globalisation, has led to a profits bonanza for big business and a prolonged economic upswing in the USA and Europe.

On the other hand, Information Technology doesn't actually produce anything. It does generate demand for computers and associated products. But these in turn are manufactured in factories by assembly-line workers. They are transported around countries and continents by lorry drivers. They are shipped between countries and continents by seafarers.

Without the labourers who dig up the roads and lay the cables, there would be no Internet. These billions of miles of cables and wiring also have to be manufactured in factories by workers. Without technicians to connect and maintain these cables, the Internet would soon cease to function.

Without power workers, oil workers, miners, and other employees in the energy-generating industries, there would be no computers because there would be no electricity. The offices which house the computers' work are not constructed on the screen of an Apple Mac, they are built by joiners, glaziers, labourers, bricklayers, painters, and a multitude of other construction workers.

Bins can't be emptied by computers, fires can't be fought over the Internet, and no software program that will ever be devised could possibly replace doctors, nurses, midwives, and other health workers.

Without farmers and fishermen, without waiters and waitresses, the new intellectual, business, and cultural elite would be unable to enjoy expensive meals in upmarket restaurants. Nor could they travel by road, sea, air, or rail, because none of these systems could be run or maintained without transport workers. And without water and sewage workers, the new intellectual elite would eventually be wiped out by disease.

Some commentators predict that eventually online shopping will replace, or at least seriously undermine, the entire retail trade. But even online shopping requires drivers and postal workers to deliver the goods that are purchased by email.

Yet there are important grains of truth in Professor Angell's apocalyptic projections. Huge swathes of businesses face the prospect of total wipe-out as the information revolution accelerates. Skilled and unskilled jobs will be wiped out in their hundreds of millions across the Northern Hemisphere. Sectors such as banking and finance will be especially vulnerable with some analysts calculating that, within a decade or so, 150,000 banking jobs in the UK will be wiped out.

This would have an especially devastating effect on Scotland's main financial centre, Edinburgh, which could eventually suffer the fate that its West Coast neighbour suffered back in the late 1970s and early 1980s. Heavy industry fled Glasgow during that time, and the resulting collapse of the economy has left behind a terrible legacy of poverty and deprivation which endures to this day.

As online shopping becomes more popular, employment in the retail industry and in the packaging industry, which is largely geared towards making products recognisable on the retail shelves, is likely to be decimated.

Call centres, which now employ 35,000 people in Scotland, are especially vulnerable to the onslaught of online services. Even the pitifully low-paid jobs in the fast-food shops are likely to vanish as McDonald's, Burger King, Kentucky Fried Chicken, and the rest of the big franchises switch to computerised vending machines.

The provision of online services at the cheapest rates is also likely to lead to the collapse of many smaller businesses which employ reasonably well-paid workers. One online company now offers printing services to any company or organisation anywhere in the world, from design right through to distribution, at cheaper prices than any established printers could hope to match.

There is no possibility that these jobs will be replaced by new hi-tech jobs in the computer and electronics industries. Scotland's Silicon Glen, for example, today employs just 30,000 people, which is 10,000 fewer than it employed 20 years ago.

Nine out of ten of these jobs consist of desperately low-paid soul-destroying assembly-line work. Back in 1996, a BBC documentary, *Frontline Scotland*, revealed that Scotland's electronics workers had the lowest pay, the longest hours, and the worst conditions of any electronics workers in the developed world. Almost half had a take-home pay of under £160 for a 44-hour week. Conditions today in 'Sweatshop Glen' are no better.[7]

Politicians and economists frequently speak in awe-stricken tones about the miraculous Silicon Valley in California. They conjure up images of a vast belt of affluence, where hundreds of thousands of workers drive home in expensive cars every evening from their gleaming hi-tech offices to their plush detached villas.

The real Silicon Valley bears no resemblance to this mythical wonderland. Most of the workforce are black or Hispanic and live in abject poverty. At $8 an hour, the wages are higher than in Silicon Glen. But in that part of the US, the cost of living is so exorbitant that it can cost an entire month's salary to rent a single-apartment flat.

Meanwhile, software companies like Microsoft have emerged as the all-powerful global giants of the early 21st century. But they do not generate employment. The combined workforce of Microsoft, Oracle, and Computer Associates – the three largest software companies in America – is less than one tenth the total workforce of the largest car company, General Motors. A new company set up in Britain by BT, the Bank of Scotland, and a computer software company is poised to dominate the market in international telephone calls by offering a combination of advanced computer technology and cheaper phone calls. The company, Quip, has its headquarters in Milton Keynes, and has a total workforce of just 15.

How different the reality of 21st-century capitalism is from the expectations of earlier generations of political leaders. Back in 1964, the newly elected Labour Prime Minister, Harold Wilson, forecast that 'the white heat of technology' would slash the length of the working week. He forecast that by the year 2000 there would be a maximum 20-hour working week as a consequence of technological progress.

Yet, 36 years on, the average blue-collar worker in Britain works four and a half hours a week longer than in 1964. White-collar workers also work longer hours and are under more stress and strain than ever before. As Psychology Professor Cary Cooper of the University of Manchester Institute for Science and Technology points out, 'We have moved into a culture of short-term contracts, job insecurity, work overload and long hours.'[8]

In the intervening period since Harold Wilson made his bold prediction, technology has advanced into the realms of what would have seemed like science fiction back then. Yet the dream of a 20-hour working week appears about as far-fetched as Dr Who's Tardis seemed to schoolchildren back in 1964.

Chapter Four

SHIFTING THE BLAME

THE BRAZILIAN ARCHBISHOP, the late Dom Camara, once made a penetrating observation which caused uproar within his own Church hierarchy, 'When I feed the poor, they call me a saint. When I ask why they are poor, they call me a communist.'

So why are they poor? New Labour thinks it knows the answer. The poor are poor, according to government Ministers, because they choose to be poor. Welfare benefits are too generous and encourage 'dependency'. That's why we have a huge 'underclass' which drains the economy dry.

'We are planning a new crackdown on the workshy,' says Chancellor Gordon Brown. 'There are job vacancies in every region of Britain and people able to work have no excuse for not filling them.'

His colleague, Alistair Darling, repeatedly threatens 'tough new penalties for the workshy'. With a flourish he declares, 'We have decided to end the something for nothing culture.' Unfortunately, he was not issuing advance notice of the pending abolition of the monarchy. His target was lone parents and disabled people. Lone mothers would now be targeted for compulsory interviews under threat of benefit withdrawal, while thousands of people on Incapacity Benefit would be forced back to work. 'Too many men in their 50s and 60s are on Incapacity Benefit when they should be working,' preached the former left-wing socialist, now a rising New Labour star.

One of these men being targeted by Alistair Darling is 55-year-old Billy, from the South Side of Glasgow. He looks after his 80-year-old invalided mother and receives £73 a week Incapacity Benefit, plus £62 Industrial Injuries Benefit. Billy left school 30 years ago and started work as an insulating engineer working with dangerous asbestos. He now has serious respiratory problems, and, like tens of thousands of men of his generation in the Clydeside area, has a high risk of contracting lung cancer because of his exposure to the poisonous mineral.

Billy later worked as a scaffold erector and spent years of his life literally inches away from plunging hundreds of feet to his death. He has also worked in the ICI plant at Grangemouth where he handled dangerous chemicals. Billy's working life ended after he was pinned against a wall by a forklift truck, which crushed the two main bones in his back like Oxo cubes. Ever since, he has suffered constant pain.[1]

Mr Darling has lived a rather different life. He attended the exclusive Loretto School on the outskirts of Edinburgh which charges £12,000 a year in fees – double the amount that Billy has to live on, six times the amount that a single unemployed person has to live on, and £4500 more than a worker on the national minimum wage will earn in a year. After leaving school, Mr Darling became a solicitor, an advocate, then a Labour MP. He is now a Cabinet Minister on a £100,000-a-year salary, plus lavish expenses. He recently tried to buy a new house in Edinburgh: a 13-room former nursing home, which eventually sold for half a million. Like most of the politicians and media pundits who pontificate about 'spiralling welfare costs' and 'the culture of dependency', Alistair Darling, designated New Labour's 'Poverty Tsar', has as much first-hand experience of poverty as he has of life on the planet Pluto.

The truth is, welfare spending is not spiralling out of control. In the last 20 years, it has risen just two and a half per cent in the UK relative to Gross Domestic Product. This is despite the fact that the population has aged dramatically during that period, the number of single-parent households has multiplied six-fold, and whole regions of the country have been reduced to a state of permanent economic depression.

Nor is it true that the Treasury coffers are being gobbled up by an army of idlers and scroungers attracted by a life of splendour on £40 a week dole payments. Only five per cent of welfare spending goes to the unemployed. A large part of the welfare budget goes to pensioners, who have worked all their lives. Another big chunk goes to people whose health has been destroyed as a result of years of heavy manual labour. And a vast amount goes to people who do work, but are paid such pitiful wages by their employers that they are forced to claim benefits to feed and clothe their families.

Blaming welfare payments for poverty or unemployment is as logical as blaming firefighters for fires, or blaming doctors for ill health. Why do unemployment levels vary from twelve per cent in the East End of Glasgow to less than two per cent in Grampian, when benefit payments are exactly the same in both parts of Scotland? How come there was a vast 'underclass' in the 1930s, when there was no welfare state? And why, after the welfare state was established following the Second World War, did the economy not collapse as multitudes of workers left their factories and offices to join the 'something for nothing brigade'? Why, indeed, did unemployment not only decrease instead, but almost cease to exist in the few decades after the welfare state was established?

It's not necessary to have a PhD in economics to work out the solutions to these questions. The simple truth is that poverty and unemployment are not caused by the poor and the unemployed – they are caused by the rich and powerful. The decisions which lead to depressions, recessions, slumps, redundancies, closures, and lay-offs aren't taken in the back streets of Easterhouse or Craigmillar – they're taken in the boardrooms of big business, by company chairmen and chief executives.

Moreover, bizarre as it may seem, the people who do take the decisions to increase poverty and unemployment are never penalised. Instead they are handsomely rewarded. For example, Jack Welch, the chief executive of the giant American multi-national, General Electric, slashed the payroll of the company by over 100,000 in eight years. He closed or sold 98 factories. But by making these savage economies, he increased the company's annual profits from $1.5 billion to $9.3 billion dollars. And, as a reward for his butchery, Mr Welch picked up almost $100 million – 2500 times the salary of the average General Electric employee.[2]

Recently, in Britain, the chief executive of Barclay's Bank, Matt Barnett, announced a 30 per cent surge in profits to just under £2.5 billion. The shareholders were naturally delighted at this windfall, which was achieved partly by axeing 7500 jobs. But Mr Barnett says he's still not satisfied. His aim now is to double the bank's profits every four years. And as the first step on the road to achieving that goal, he will cut £1 billion from costs, slash thousands more jobs and close down hundreds of High Street branches.

To the workforce of Barclay's, who delivered that 30 per cent profit increase, Mr Barnett warns 'there will be no excuses, no sacred cows, no delusions'.

He will be demanding, he says, 'a more rigorous value-based management framework', which is business gobbledygook for insisting that the remaining staff work even harder to make even fatter profits for the shareholders.[3]

Here in Scotland, the directors of the Royal Bank of Scotland have pledged to wipe out 20,000 jobs, following their triumphant takeover of the Nat West Bank. The top executives will no doubt be handsomely rewarded for their business acumen. They will receive bonuses equal to a lifetime's salary for the average Royal Bank employee. They can possibly even expect knighthoods and other baubles and titles from the government. Yet by sacking 20,000 staff, the management of the Royal Bank is likely to cost the taxpayer up to £150 million, including the cost of welfare benefits and lost tax revenues.

In the Third World, the corporate godfathers perpetrate some of the most abominable crimes against humanity imaginable, to drive up profit margins. Impoverished states are stripped bare of their natural resources. Workers are turned into industrial and agricultural slaves. Farmers are ruthlessly ripped off and governments have guns held to their heads by transnational companies demanding that trade unions are outlawed, public services are dismantled, and tax rates lowered.

Glasgow-based tea-producing company, James Finlay, employs 51,000 workers across the globe in its vast tea plantations. The average wage per employee of the company in 1996 was £772, or £14 a week.[4] When you buy a jar of coffee sold in a supermarket for £3.00, just 15 pence goes to the farmer in the tropics who produces the coffee bean. The rest is ripped off by giant companies like Nestlé and Allied Lyons and by supermarkets like Asda and Sainsbury. When you buy a bunch of bananas, 90 per cent of the cash you pay goes to the supermarket and to multinationals like Chiquita and Del Monte, who control the trade. When you buy a bar of chocolate for 45 pence, the farmer in Ghana who produces the cocoa bean will be paid a quarter of a penny.[5]

Despite the mountain of evidence condemning these corporate mercenaries, New Labourites and old Tories alike grovel at their feet and encourage them to pile up even more profit and cause even more unemployment and poverty.

Speaking at the 2000 World Economic Forum in Davos, Tony Blair exhorted other European states to follow in the footsteps of the UK by liberalising markets, slashing state subsidies, and cutting back social regulation – in other words, by creating the best possible conditions for big business to make the biggest possible profits. Writing in *Scotland on Sunday*, New Labour guru John Lloyd explained the logic behind this Thatcherite vision: 'New Labour wants capitalism to be dynamic – to produce the kind of surpluses which they can tax sufficiently to protect the losers.'[6]

We're back again to the trickle-down theory – and it's as bankrupt under New Labour as it was under Margaret Thatcher. While the poor need coercion and threats to force them out of poverty, the rich require incentives and inducements to entice them to make even more money. New Labour's method of protecting the losers is nothing else if not unorthodox. 'We're making sure penalties for the unemployed will be harsher,' said one government adviser quoted in the London *Times*.[7]

Meanwhile, capitalism *is* producing surpluses, monumental surpluses, the biggest surpluses in the whole of history. But New Labour is *not* 'taxing them sufficiently to protect the losers'. Indeed, New Labour boasts that corporation tax on big business and capital gains tax on the rich is 'the lowest in Europe'.[8] The UK government has even blocked the modest proposal of other European governments for a 'withholding tax' on capital being moved across borders.

According to a Joseph Rowntree Foundation study published in December 1999, despite the booming stock exchange at that time, the number of people on very low incomes in Britain had increased by a million during the first two years of the New Labour government. While big business in Scotland and across the UK has amassed record profits, the proportion of children claiming free school meals and clothing grants in Glasgow's schools is higher today than on the day Tony Blair entered Downing Street.

The Labour Party no longer talks about building a society based on equality. Instead, Tony Blair, with all the sincerity of a Mafia defence lawyer, produces an agonised expression and pledges to create a society of 'equality of opportunity'. But 'equality of opportunity' is not equality. The National Lottery offers 'equality of opportunity'. Everyone has the same chance of becoming a millionaire as everyone else. But, as we all know in our heart of hearts, even as we queue up in the post office on a Saturday morning, there is more chance of being struck by lightning than of becoming a millionaire by buying a lottery ticket. Still, as millions wait patiently for their giros or pensions to arrive, they can always console themselves with the knowledge that they're actually participating in an equal-opportunities project.

As a matter of fact, society under New Labour does not even provide the same equal opportunity as the National Lottery. How can everyone have an equal opportunity when some people inherit vast amounts of wealth on the day they're born? How can there be a society based on equal opportunity when there are fee-paying schools – open only to the children of wealthy parents – which virtually guarantee pupils entry to a top university? How can there be equal opportunity when students from working-class families have to work long hours in bars or call centres to pay their way through university while trying to study for exams? How can there be equal opportunity when many children live in damp, overcrowded homes with nowhere to do their homework or even to read in peace?

The long-term goal of New Labour is to transform Britain into a smaller version of the USA. Tony Blair regularly heaps glowing praise on 'the American economic miracle', which, he claims, 'has created millions of jobs'. It may have created millions of jobs in the past ten years, as a result of the longest economic upswing in the country's history, but it is a startling fact that there are now more people in the USA living in poverty today than there were a decade ago.

There are now 35.5 million Americans officially defined as poor, including 27 per cent of black and Hispanics and 23 per cent of all children. In New York, the richest city of the richest country of the world, a baby born today is more likely to die in its first year and has a lower life expectancy than a baby born in Shanghai.[9]

Even after almost a decade of economic upswing, the USA is now a more divided, unequal, and repressive society than the former semi-fascist concentration camps of Chile or Argentina. While stocks, shares, profits, and dividends have soared to previously unimaginable heights, 80 per cent of Americans have suffered either a fall or stagnation in their living standards. Even if the economy continues to grow, economists calculate that another 2.5 million people will descend into poverty within the next two years.[10]

It is true that new jobs have been created in America. But these are different from the jobs that have been 'downsized' by the big corporations or exported to the Third World. Overwhelmingly, the new jobs are the sweatshop jobs, which offer wages and conditions that no-one would have accepted in the past. But people have to accept them now, because the alternative is starvation.

In New York, if someone loses their workfare job, they get evicted from their homeless shelter. Women who lose their workfare job have their children taken into care. In San Francisco, workfare street sweepers are paid one third of trade-union rates and have their benefits docked if they are ten minutes late for a shift that starts at 6.30 am.[11]

Meanwhile, five million people in the USA, equivalent to the total population of Scotland, are either incarcerated in prison or are on probation. In the richest country in the world, which has just experienced the most prolonged period of economic growth in history, one person in 100 is in jail. This compares to one in 1000 in Britain, which in turn is the highest in Europe apart from Turkey.[12]

'I have seen the future and it works,' said the famous American journalist, Lincoln Steffens when he visited Russia in 1917. Tony Blair has seen the future for Britain in Washington, New York, and Los Angeles. It certainly works for the rich. It doesn't work for the poor.

And therein lies the answer to the question posed by Archbishop Camara. The poor are poor and are growing poorer . . . because the rich are rich and are growing richer.

Part Two

WATCHING THE WHEELS GO ROUND

Ah, people asking questions lost in confusion
Well I tell them there's no problems, only solutions.

Chapter Five

THE GLOBAL MONEY MACHINE

'THE ONE AND only responsibility of business is to make as much money as possible for its shareholders.' The honesty and clarity of this statement, by economist Milton Friedman, the guru of Thatcherism, leaves no room for misunderstanding.[1]

Friedman, hailed by the rich and powerful across the globe as the greatest economic philosopher of the 20th century, doesn't try to pull the wool over anyone's eyes by pretending that capitalism could ever have a social conscience. In fact, he explicitly denounces the idea that businesses should display any social responsibility to the wider community, the environment or the workforce as 'a fundamentally subversive doctrine'.[2]

When he makes this observation, Milton Friedman is not just voicing an opinion, he is stating a fact. Some well-meaning politicians and writers would like big business to behave more honourably. But asking corporate capitalism to behave humanely is like asking a stone statue to shed tears. That's not because the bosses that run the business empires are necessarily malevolent by nature – although undoubtedly the corporate boardrooms contain more than their share of strutting would-be Mussolinis.

But there are others who profess to be sincere followers of the carpenter of Nazareth who – if even some of the tales of his life are true – was an early revolutionary who stood up for the poor and downtrodden against the Roman Empire and its henchmen.

In the gospel of Saint Luke he is quoted as saying, 'It is easier for a camel to go through the eye of a needle than for a rich man to enter into the Kingdom of God.'

One rich man who believes that he will enter the Kingdom of God is Scotland's wealthiest man, Brian Souter. A member of the fundamentalist Baptist sect, the Church of the Nazarene, Mr Souter feels so strongly about his Christian beliefs that he recently threatened to spend the whole of his vast fortune fighting to keep Section 28, which prevents teachers from acknowledging the existence of homosexuality. If necessary, he explained, he would 'go back and live in council house' in order to stop this iniquitous plot to corrupt the minds of young children.

This is a man whose religion clearly dominates his whole life. Except where it comes to business, that is. Here, the Stagecoach boss's behaviour is not quite in the spirit of the man who drove the moneylenders out of the temple 2000 years ago. Mr Souter's business empire was built by driving competitors out of business, slashing wages and sacking workers. But, as the devout transport tycoon explains, 'If we were to apply the Sermon on the Mount to our business we would be rooked within six months. Don't misunderstand me, ethics are not irrelevant – but some are incompatible with what we have to do because capitalism is based on greed.'[3]

Then there's the chief executive of the German multinational, Continental, which makes tyres. In an interview with *Business Week*, Hubertus von Grunberg described the anguish he faces every time he has to lay off workers.

'Our Irish workers were good to us and now they're no longer with us,' he says after closing the only tyre factory in Ireland. He goes on, 'The workers we lost in Austria and East Germany – they were loyal workers. They didn't stage strikes, they came in on Saturdays when we needed them. They have been good and loyal . . . they have not caused a recall in 30 years because they made a quality product. And all of a sudden you can't pay them any more.'[4]

Reading this interview, it's hard to fight back the tears of sympathy for this poor creature. So angst-ridden is he at the role he has been forced to play – presumably at gunpoint – that he cannot even bear to use words such as 'sacked' or 'fired'. Instead he talks of the Irish workers being 'no longer with us', which gives the impression that they've died, and of the Austrian workers being 'lost', as though they simply disappeared one morning.

So why exactly are these workers 'lost' or 'no longer with us'? Mr von Grunberg explains: 'I cannot defend making products [in these countries] with my shareholders. The shareholders will ask me, "well it's so much better to make products in the Czech Republic and other cheap labour areas. Why don't you make it all there?" It's a difficult balancing act, and I would rather not have to do it. It's not an attractive job.'[5]

Two years later, and Continental, under Mr von Grunberg, had doubled its profits and its shares were soaring. At the company's Scottish plant, wages had been slashed by seven per cent and hours increased from 39 to 42. Then, all of a sudden, the Continental bosses decided to make their Scottish workforce 'disappear'. They announced the closure of their factory on the outskirts of Edinburgh. A thousand Scottish workers were thrown on the dole and production was shifted to Romania, where wage bills are much lower.

The name of the game these days is globalisation. It's not exactly a new idea. As billionaire currency speculator and business guru George Soros has pointed out, 'Its main features were first identified in rather prophetic fashion by Karl Marx and Frederick Engels in the *Communist Manifesto*, published in 1848.' Soros goes on to make a telling point: 'Marx and Engels gave a very good analysis of the capitalist system 150 years ago, better in some ways, I may say, than classical economics.'[6]

From the mid 19th century up until 1914, the global capitalist economy was based on the technology of underwater telegraph cables and steamships. These gigantic scientific advances linked the world together as it had never been linked before. Along with a meteoric explosion in world trade, that period also marked the heyday of military imperialism, when rich, powerful countries such as Britain and the USA marauded across the planet, physically conquering and occupying poorer countries and robbing them of their resources.

The legendary American folk singer Woody Guthrie once sang 'Some will rob you with a six-gun, others with a fountain pen.' These days, the weapons of imperialist robbery are more likely to be computers and telephones rather than tanks and battleships and, as a general rule – although there are always exceptions to every rule – the robberies are carried out not by governments, but by giant transnational corporations.

The sheer speed and scale of the interconnections that now link the planet together would have been incomprehensible at the beginning of the last century. These technological changes have smashed down borders and barriers between states and paved the way for the emergence of the new corporate superpowers who shift wealth around the world at the speed of sound.

Globalisation is essentially two simultaneous races. In one of these races, the participants are the giant companies of the world. Their performances are measured by the amount of profits they can pile up. The ultimate goal of each of these companies is to achieve total global domination in their sphere.

The other race involves not corporations but nation-states. But unlike a normal race, which aims to achieve the highest standards possible, this race between nations is a race to achieve the *lowest* standards possible. You'll get the general picture if you imagine a football league table where the winners are not the team that achieves the most victories and scores the most goals but the side that suffers the most defeats and *concedes* the most goals. The nations that can achieve the harshest working conditions, the lowest wages, the most ruthless forms of exploitation, the longest hours, the most threadbare public services, the most polluted environments, are the winners.

While the race involving the global corporations is a race to the top, the other race, involving the national states, is a race to the bottom. Almost every government in the world has filled in its entry form, and there is no more enthusiastic participant in this race than Great Britain. But the UK still has a long way to go before it catches up with the front runners in the race towards national destitution.

A century ago, millions of workers across Central Scotland, the north of Ireland, and northern England toiled their lives away in Dickensian factories which belched poisonous fumes into the atmosphere for semi-starvation wages. These factories have not gone away. They still exist more or less as they did at the time of Dickens, except that they've been exported to Jakarta, Bombay, Mexico City, and a hundred other Third World cities, where 80 per cent of the world's industrial workforce now live. Most of the goods that people use to live their daily lives – clothing, shoes, TVs, watches, toys, jewellery – are now made in these cities of the Southern Hemisphere where wages are low, trade-union rights non-existent, and working conditions akin to the visions of hell described by Alexander Cordell in his novels set in South Wales in the early days of the Industrial Revolution.

In many Bangkok factories, young women from the country-side are conscripted to work 18 hours a day stitching shirts. They are forced to eat and sleep in the factories in which they work. Their drinking water is spiked with amphetamines to make them work harder, faster, and longer.[7]

In factories across the Ear East, young women are sexually abused as a matter of course. Employees are even locked up in factories to save the companies employing supervisors. In one such factory in Bangkok a few years ago, 200 workers burned to death.

Where the multinationals have moved in, local environments are desecrated beyond recognition. Fertile landscapes are converted into deserts. Rivers, seas, and lakes are turned into toxic reservoirs. Disease runs rampant. But the beauty of globalisation is that it allows the millionaires and billionaires who own the means of production – the factories, the natural resources, the machinery, the computers, the offices – to become even more fabulously wealthy.

The global marketplace is in effect a worldwide market, not for goods, but for cheap labour. It is like a colossal hi-tech international version of the hiring fairs of rural Ireland at the end of the 19th century, as described in the novels and poems of the Donegalborn writer, Patrick McGill, the 'Navvy Poet':

> 'Since two can't gain in the bargain,
> Then who shall bear the loss,
> When little children are auctioned
> As slaves at the Market Cross?
> Come to the Cross and the Market,
> Where the wares of the world are sold,
> And the wares are little children,
> Traded for pieces of gold.'[8]

A BBC2 documentary a few years ago, *The Hollow State*, looked at how one company, which manufactures polythene bags, closed a factory in the UK and shifted its operation to China. The company now imports the raw polythene into China, turns it into plastic carrier bags, then exports tens of millions of them back to Britain for use in supermarkets. Any transport costs are more than cancelled out by the fact that workers in China are paid £100 a month for a 42-hour week – one tenth of the wages of those who were sacked in Britain.[9] Across industry as a whole, the same pattern is repeated over and over again. The process began on a modest scale back in the 1970s, with American companies opening factories in the so-called 'developing countries' of Latin America and East Asia. Car factories in Brazil were staffed by shanty-town dwellers who could never dream of ever affording to buy any of the cars they built. Most of these cars were exported back to the USA.

But now even the semi-developed countries like Brazil and the Philippines are being spurned by the transnationals as they search for even cheaper labour and even lower rates of taxation. Over the past decade or so, Nike, the American sportswear giant, has flitted from the US to South Korea, to Indonesia and now to Vietnam in a never-ending quest for cheaper labour, lower production costs, and higher profits.

The company's supply factories employ around 80,000 workers, mainly young women, churning out running shoes for export to the West. Their average wage last year worked out at the equivalent of around £15 a month, which means they would have to save every penny of their wages for five months before they could actually buy a pair of Nike Air running shoes.

Some researchers estimate that, of the £60 you pay in the shops for a pair of running shoes, the 40 workers who produced that shoe in the Far East will have been paid not much more than £1 among them. Even taking into account raw materials and overheads, a running shoe will cost no more than a tenner to produce, which means the sportswear companies and the retailer are making a handsome killing on every pair sold.[10]

Some corporations have dragged the hunt for cheap labour down to an even lower level. Major American airlines, for example, are now employing prisoners serving life sentences for murder to operate telesales services.[11]

The insatiable quest by corporate capitalism for higher profits involves more than just a search for the countries that offer the lowest wages, otherwise Rwanda would be the top destination for transnational capitalism. In their battle to attract inward investment, governments also have to offer extra financial inducements, such as grants, concessions, subsidies, and low rates of taxation.

On top of that, big business requires an infrastructure, including roads, railways, airports, ports, water, electricity, and telecommunications. It also looks for a reasonably educated workforce, able to cope with modern industrial techniques, which means at least a basic level of literacy and numeracy.

But neither infrastructure nor education costs are paid for by the transnational corporations. They are provided free of charge by governments, which generate the funds by deducting taxes from the meagre wages that have attracted the multinationals to come in the first place.

At this stage, the flight of industry to the Southern Hemisphere has mainly involved traditional manufacturing industries. But increasingly, hi-tech companies too are looking southwards. In India, some computer programmers earn as little £2000 a year, or £40 a week.[12] Economists calculate that within a generation there will be millions of trained engineers, scientists, computer programmers, software writers, data analysts, and other professional experts prepared to work for a fraction of the wages of the workforces of Europe and America.

In addition, the former Soviet Union and Eastern Europe can offer a highly educated workforce prepared to work for rock-bottom rates of pay, an alluring combination for the corporate vultures. As these Eastern European states sign up for the European Union, the writing will begin to appear on the wall of the hundreds of electronics factories across Central Scotland that make up Silicon Glen. American and Asian investment in these plants (and in similar plants in South Wales and southern Ireland) has been motivated, in part at least, by the need to gain access to the lucrative European Union marketplace.

As technology advances, the balance of power shifts even more decisively in favour of the giant transnational corporations. For example, Ford UK, the British arm of the American car multi-national, has recently announced that it will buy its components online, rather than from local supply industries. In practice, it will mean that the company can trawl the Internet searching for the cheapest suppliers of the hundreds of different parts that are required to assemble a car.

In the past, car factories and other assembly plants stimulated entire regional economies. The shipbuilding industry on the Clyde, essentially an assembly industry, generated five jobs outside the yard for every worker employed in the actual construction of a ship. In its heyday, shipbuilding employed upwards of 100,000 people – but hundreds of thousands more were employed in local engineering factories which supplied the yards. Now companies like Ford can buy in, for instance, windscreens from China, upholstery from Indonesia, brake discs from the Philippines, and so on. Meanwhile, local supply industries topple like skittles.

Some right-wing economists, mesmerised by statistics showing profits surging, stock markets booming, and technology advancing fantasise that we are living a 'New Economy', in which all the old problems of recessions and slumps, unemployment and inflation, strikes and political discontent, have become as outdated as cloth caps and tacket boots

Professor Donald MacKay, the former chief of Scottish Enterprise, claims that 'the effects of globalisation, spread about with the aid of the advanced countries, will address world poverty'.[13]

Unfortunately for the billions who actually suffer poverty, the eminent professor is living in Disneyland. The truth is that, far from exporting prosperity to the Third World, globalisation is importing Third World poverty into the First World.

The ships that were once built on the Clyde are now built by cheap labour on the Yangtse, while once-thriving shipbuilding communities are turned into post-industrial wastelands. The textile mills in the Borders fall silent and empty, their work taken over by industrial concentration camps in Jakarta and Manila. From Clydebank to Selkirk and scores of towns in between, the price of globalisation is mass long-term unemployment.

So far, the full brutal consequences of globalisation have been partly masked by the economic upswing of the past eight years, which has generated millions of low-paid service jobs across the Northern Hemisphere. But, as author John Katz, an investment expert who edits *Portfolio 2000*, points out, 'What goes up must come down'. Katz goes on to predict 'a nosebleed-inducing dive and a very hard landing indeed'.

Similarly, the influential *American Business Week* magazine warns that 'sooner, rather than later, the new economy boom is likely to be followed by a new economy bust – a recession and stockmarket decline which could be much deeper than most people expect'.[14]

The reason for this 'business cycle' of upswing-downswing, recovery-recession, boom-bust, was laid bare more than a century ago by Karl Marx. In a system based on the exploitation of labour for private profit, the workforce cannot be paid enough to buy the goods they produce, otherwise there would be no profit for the shareholders.

On a global scale, more goods are made than the population of the world can afford. Every so often, vast surpluses pile up which cannot be sold for profit. As a result, the stock market plummets, profits turn into losses, businesses fail, factories close, workers are sacked, unemployment grows, and, for a period of time, there is a general contraction of industry and trade.

That's exactly what happened a few years ago to the Asian Tigers of the Far East. One day economists and politicians across the globe, including Tony Blair, were drooling over 'the Asian economic miracle'. Then all of sudden the wine turned back into water. The entire region was dragged into recession and the subsequent social turmoil ended the 32-year reign of President Suharto of Indonesia.

In America and Europe, recession has been staved off temporarily by new technology and globalisation, in much the same way that a hangover can be delayed by drinking another bottle of wine. But eventually everything catches up, and the economic hangover that will follow the current consumer binge is likely be to severe indeed.

If anything the new globalised economy based on superprofiteering and ultra-exploitation is even more fragile and unstable than traditional capitalism. Back in the days when Henry Ford launched his T-model Ford, his assembly workers were paid $750 a year. It would have taken two years' wages for these American workers to buy a Ford car. Today, many Latin American and Asian car assembly workers are paid around $1000, and would have to work for 15 years to buy one of the cars they make.

In every sector of the global economy, the same gulf exists between wages and prices. In the sportswear industry, for example, there are an estimated one billion pairs of unsold training shoes, or one for every six people in the world.

Eventually, the billions of products being churned out daily in factories and assembly plants across the world will saturate the world markets, leading to a new downward spiral. No-one can predict the exact day, week, month, or even year when this will occur. Nor can we anticipate how long a new recession will last, or how steep it will be, or the political repercussions that will flow from it. But one thing is certain: when this orgy of profiteering turns sour, it won't be the profiteers who caused the crisis who will pay the price for that crisis.

Chapter Six

WHO WRITES THE RULES?

JUST AFTER THE first Scottish Parliamentary elections, journalist and cultural commentator, Pat Kane, wrote a column in the *Sunday Herald* newspaper in which he described himself as 'a democratic capitalist'.

The revelation that a key member of the editorial staff of one of Scotland's leading liberal newspapers describes himself as a 'democratic capitalist' doesn't exactly qualify as the scoop of the decade. Yet, until recently, Kane, who first rose to fame as the lead singer of the band Hue and Cry, was proud to identify himself as a socialist.

Unlike many other intellectuals in the media and in politics who have forsaken their earlier beliefs in socialism and made their peace with the system, Pat Kane is no foaming-at-the-mouth reactionary. His writings are socially progressive on most issues. His commitment to democracy cannot be doubted.

There is, however, one fatal flaw at the heart of his new philosophy. The phrase 'democratic capitalist' is a contradiction in terms. It is no more possible to be a democratic capitalist than it is to be a meat-eating vegetarian.

Some people may think that's a bit harsh. After all, in this country we've been brought up saturated with the spirit of democracy. A generation still alive today fought in a World War to defend democracy against Nazism. We have the right to vote, the right to strike, the right to worship as we please, the right to free speech, the right to join whatever political party we choose. What more could we ask for?

It's true that in Western Europe we possess a whole range of democratic rights. The achievement of the right to vote, the right to strike, the right to organise, the right to free speech were monumental advances. Without these basic democratic rights most of the population would still be living in squalid slums and working in dark Satanic mills for a pittance. More than anyone, socialists value democratic rights and will fight ferociously to protect them.

But these democratic rights were not handed out like Christmas presents by the capitalist rulers of society. Each and every one of them had to be fought for long and hard. The Chartists of the early 19th century, for example, were furiously denounced by the politicians, the businessmen, the press, and the clergy. Their central demand – the right to vote – was regarded as an outlandishly revolutionary proposal by those in charge. In the early 20th century, the Suffragettes, too, were vilified as dangerous extremists threatening the very fabric of society.

Moreover, a handful of democratic rights don't add up to a democracy, any more than a handful of trees add up to a forest. Abraham Lincoln once defined democracy as 'government of the people, by the people, for the people'. That's certainly what the ancient Greeks, who invented the word, meant by democracy. Translated into English, democracy means, literally, 'rule by the people'.

Under capitalism, rule by the people is a political impossibility. Even elected governments have only limited powers over certain areas of government. In his book *The Cancer Stage of Capitalism*, John McMurtry quotes a top New York banker who told a radio interviewer, 'We are like the supranational government of the world. Where we see politicians are doing things that are inappropriate, we hold their feet to the fire. And the way we do that is by moving a lot of money around. Politicians are irrelevant to the process.'

The real economic rulers of the world today won't be found in parliaments or in presidential palaces. It is in the boardrooms of the big corporations and on the floors of the world's stock exchanges that most of the key decisions are taken that affect the lives of ordinary people.

A company like General Electric employs 350,000 people in over 100 companies. Its annual revenues are greater than Scotland's total Gross Domestic Product. It produces a mind-boggling range of products, from aircraft engines to computer disks, from X-ray equipment to nuclear power stations. It owns 220 different media subsidiaries including 13 TV stations in America, dozens of cable channels in 54 different countries, and scores of radio stations and Internet channels. It controls a vast empire of insurance companies, and even controls a number of top American sports teams and venues, including Madison Square Garden.[1]

Yet this whole operation is run by one man, John F Welch. He is just one of 1000 corporate chieftains who have become the 21st-century equivalent of the feudal kings and queens, except that their domain knows no geographical boundaries.

They have the power to destroy lives, impoverish communities, and topple governments without even leaving their offices. And they are accountable to no-one, except unelected boards of directors.

The power of these business moguls is reinforced by three giant institutions which together effectively act as the political wing of transnational capitalism. This gang of three – the World Trade Organisation, the World Bank, and the International Monetary Fund – work together to force national governments to accept ultra-right-wing free-market policies. They have forbidden governments to ban dangerous asbestos. They have forbidden countries to ban child labour. They have forbidden countries to ban trade with vicious dictatorships such as Burma. They have forbidden countries to produce cheap generic medicines, forcing them to buy instead expensive brands manufactured by the big drugs companies. They have demanded that countries slash public spending, reduce labour costs, and privatise public assets.

So who exactly are these institutions? When were they were elected? Who are they accountable to? In theory, they represent the 188 members of the United Nations. In practice, the seven richest countries – the so-called G7 – have the same number of votes as the other 181 countries combined.

Not many people in Britain have ever heard of Stephen Pickford. It would be fair to say he's hardly a household name, even in his own household. He has never stood for public election in his life. Yet Mr Pickford is Britain's representative on the World Bank and on the IMF. He was not even appointed by the Westminster parliament to these positions, nor is he accountable to parliament. In fact, incredible as it may seem, Stephen Pickford casts his vote, which amounts to five per cent of the total voting power on these bodies, in complete secrecy.

Political and economic power go hand in hand at every level of capitalist society, from the giant global institutions right down to local health boards and council services. In Scotland, for example, just 75,000 people – less than one in 50 of the adult population – earn more than £40,000 a year.[2] Yet every MSP and MP, every senior civil servant, every senior editor of every national newspaper, every top TV and radio executive, every sheriff, every judge, every senior police officer, every major company director, every health board chief, every top council official, every quango boss in Scotland earns £40,000 and upwards. Indeed, most of them earn much, much more.

This means that the people who run Scotland – its economy, its media, its social services, its legal system, its governmental apparatus – are drawn from the wealthiest two per cent of the population. The other 98 per cent are effectively excluded from the running of society.

In his book *Friends in High Places*, *Newsnight* presenter Jeremy Paxman pointed out that seven out of the nine top army generals, two thirds of the directors of the Bank of England, 33 of 39 of Britain's top judges, 100 per cent of ambassadors to the 15 most important countries in the world, 78 of the 84 Lord Lieutenants to the Queen, and the majority of the Bishops of the Church of England were educated at a handful of top private schools.

Paxman quotes the then Provost of Eton, Lord Charteris, who explains how society really functions in our modern parliamentary democracy: 'The world is run on knowing the right people, actually. I'm sorry, but it is. Generations ago, if you were an old Etonian, if you were a member of the aristocracy, you knew the right people. Well, it's just the same now, really. It's just a lot bigger.'[3]

The rest of us have the right to vote every five years for an MP. We also have the right to elect MSPs and councillors every four years. That is clearly preferable to living under a totalitarian dictatorship. But even these elections are effectively rigged in favour of the parties that defend the status quo.

Earlier this year Brian Souter, the richest man in Scotland, splashed out £1 million in an attempt to stop the scrapping of Section 28, the law which bans teachers from acknowledging the existence of homosexuality. Labour politicians furiously condemned this use of wealth to buy political influence.

But that's how politics works under capitalism. The food industry, the pharmaceuticals industry, the tobacco industry, the alcohol industry, and all major industries, for that matter, shell out mind-blowing sums of money to influence government policy. When Margaret Thatcher was forced to step down as

Prime Minister, she became a £1 million-a-year lobbyist on behalf of the tobacco industry.

But at least our electoral system is fair. Or is it? Yes, it's fair all right – in the same way that professional football is fair. All football teams play by the same rules. Each team consists of eleven players. The goalposts are exactly the same height and width. The pitch is more or less the same size at all grounds. On the face of it, every club should have an equal chance of success. But some clubs have a more equal chance than others. In Scotland, Celtic and Rangers have colossal wealth and resources, while teams like Cowdenbeath and Clydebank are run on a shoestring. As a result, the game is overwhelmingly weighted in favour of the wealthy clubs. Politics, too, is biased in favour of those parties who have plenty of cash to spend on leaflets, posters, full-time staff, offices, computers, press, and TV advertising.

In the past, big business channelled substantial sums of money into the coffers of the Tory Party. The Labour Party was financed by the trade unions. It still is, but increasingly, Britain's multimillionaires are switching to New Labour. Others support the Lib Dems. Some even back the SNP. These political donations are never straightforward acts of philanthropy; there are always conditions. And the first condition that big business will always insist upon is that wealth itself is untouchable. This means that any party that stands even for modest redistribution of wealth is starved of resources. It may be allowed to compete in elections, but it can never hope to generate the same amount of cash to fight these elections as the pro-big-business parties.

That doesn't mean that the pro-Establishment parties will always win. Sometimes a team like Inverness Caley or Berwick Rangers can take on and defeat the might of Celtic or Rangers against all odds. And socialists too can defeat the big-business parties, even on a playing field which is about as level as the north face of Ben Nevis. But while Rangers or Celtic may be prepared to accept defeat gracefully, big business and the rich are unlikely to give up their power and wealth quite so willingly. The coach of a losing football team may well just shrug his shoulders and prepare for next season or for the next tournament. But those who own and control society will rewrite the rules over and over again before they will concede defeat.

The monarchy, for example is not simply a decoration or a tourist attraction. Nor are our MPs and MSPs forced to swear an oath of allegiance to the monarchy for purely ceremonial purposes. To those who overthrew the monarchy in France more than 200 years ago this would have seemed utterly bizarre, but in 21st-century Britain, rather than the hereditary monarch being accountable to the elected government, the elected government is accountable to the hereditary monarch.

The reigning monarch has 'reserve powers' to dismiss governments. We are led to believe that these reserve powers are simple formalities, traditions that have been retained for purely sentimental reasons. In fact, they've been used within living memory. In 1975, the Queen's governor-general in Australia sacked the Labour Prime Minister, Gough Whitlam, who had been elected three years earlier and had introduced a whole series of reforms, including the abolition of conscription, equal pay for women, increased pensions, benefits, education and health spending, and had replaced 'God Save the Queen' with 'Advance Australia Fair' as the country's national anthem.

Recently there has been much press speculation about the possibility of the Queen spending six months of the year in Holyrood Palace, of Prince Charles forging a higher profile north of the border, of Princess Anne being anointed Princess of Scotland, of Prince William attending a Scottish university. No-one should imagine that all of this attention is being lavished on Scotland because the Royal Family have decided they like our climate or our scenery. The fact is that the British ruling class are preparing contingency plans for the possible future break-up of the United Kingdom.

At some stage, the British Establishment may be forced to concede formal independence, for example, in the event that an SNP-led government in Holyrood called and won a referendom. But they will battle desperately to ensure that the Queen or another member of the Royal Family is appointed head of state of an independent Scotland as a bulwark to defend the power, privileges, and profits of the rich.

Ken Livingstone, now Mayor of London, once wrote a book called *If Voting Could Ever Change Anything, They'd Abolish It*, and as the old saying goes, there's many a true word spoken in jest. Ultimately, the wealthy minority at the top of society will defend the status quo by whatever means necessary.

For the past 50 years or so, the rule of the rich has not been under serious threat in Britain. Although there has been the occasional Labour government to deal with, as a general rule, the ruling Establishment has been able to tame these governments by a combination of bullying and bribery.

On the one side, Labour leaders are bought off with lavish salaries, plush limousines, and all the trappings of wealth and success. The legendary left-wing Labour MP, Nye Bevan once described the pomp and ceremony of the House of Commons as a form of 'ancestor worship'. From the day they walk in the door of Westminster or Holyrood, MPs and MSPs are flattered and patronised and made to feel part of a ruling Establishment. They are also awarded lavish lifestyles, which take them into a different stratosphere from the people who elect them. Even the basic salaries of backbench MPs or MSPs elevates them into the top two per cent of income earners.

On top of the £47,000 plus expenses they earn, many Westminster MPs make tens or even hundreds of thousands of pounds more from consultancies, directorships, journalism, and speaking engagements. In the early 1990s, Marc Hollingsworth, a journalist on Granada TV's *World in Action*, undertook an investigation into the world of political lobbying. He found that the House of Commons had become a 'commercial marketplace', and 384 MPs had business interests, including 552 directorships and 452 consultancies.

But just to make sure they don't step out of line, big business also browbeats elected Labour governments into submission with threats of economic chaos if they dare interfere with the vested interests of the rich. In Scotland, some financial institutions even threatened to relocate south of the border if New Labour dared to establish a Scottish Parliament. The same companies now warn that they will pull out if Scotland ever moves towards full independence.

Sometimes more extreme measures are called for. In the late 1970s, when Tony Benn was building mass support among the rank and file of the Labour Party, the respected investigative journalist Duncan Campbell was contacted by a former British Intelligence secret agent. When Campbell went to meet the agent, he was provided with a dossier of evidence which made his hair stand on end. Here, in black and white, was a plot to assassinate Tony Benn in the event that he should take over as Labour leader.

This plan to 'eliminate' Benn was no madcap scheme being touted around the ultra-right-wing fringes of British politics. In fact, at the heart of the criminal conspiracy was Airey Neave, a Tory Shadow Cabinet Minister and a close adviser to Margaret Thatcher.

While Airey Neave was still alive, the agent was too afraid to reveal his name. As a result, the magazine Duncan Campbell worked for, the *New Statesman*, held onto the story. Two years later, Airey Neave was murdered in an IRA car bomb attack and the agent was now prepared to go public. The *New*

Statesman published the revelations, but the mainstream British press imposed a total news black-out on the story.[4]

This was not the first time in recent years that a section of the British Establishment had dabbled with the idea of violently destroying an elected government. In 1968, elements of the British Establishment drew up a contingency plan to stage a military coup against Harold Wilson. Again, in 1974, just months after General Pinochet's CIA-backed coup against a democratically elected socialist government in Chile, top military officers and prominent businessmen met to discuss the possibility of taking similar action in Britain if the Labour government moved too far to the left.[5]

Their plans proved unnecessary. Under pressure from the International Monetary Fund and big business, the Labour government did what it was told. Its manifesto was torn up into small pieces and scattered to the winds, while the rich rubbed their hands with glee.

That's British democracy. It's like a rigged boxing tournament, where the fighter in the blue corner always wins and the fighter in the red corner always loses. And, if there's ever any chance that the red corner will be victorious, the referee will call the fight to a halt and declare the blue corner the winner.

Or at least that's what happens if you play by the rules laid down by the rich and powerful. That's what happened time and time again during the 20th century. And that's why, in the 21st century, we need to tear up the old rule book and establish a new set of rules.

Chapter Seven

REVOLUTION IN CYBERSPACE

THERE IS A saying in the advertising industry that 'nothing beats repetition'. If you make the same statement over and over and over again, people will start to believe it, even if it's a lie. So when an idea is repeated a million times a day across the world in newspapers, magazines, TV shows, radio programmes, and electronic bulletins, it eventually becomes difficult to resist.

Capitalism is enterprising. Capitalism is dynamic. Capitalism is innovative. Capitalism constantly revolutionises the way we live by inventing new products, new techniques, new designs. Without the swashbuckling risk-taking entrepreneurial buccaneers of the stock exchanges, human society would stagnate.

This argument is so familiar that it is rarely challenged. Most people, including even the staunchest defenders of the profit system, agree that capitalism does breed economic inequality and social injustice. But this is a modest price to pay for technological progress, we are assured. Without the incentive of competition and profit, we would not have cars, aeroplanes, TVs, computers, videos, fridges, microwave ovens, washing machines.

Most fiction is based on fact. Even children's fairy tales draw upon real life experiences. The adult fairy tale that capitalism equals dynamism and progress is not without historical foundation.

Capitalism in the early days was progressive. It swept away the restrictions and restraints of feudalism, the social system that held sway across Europe for centuries before capitalism came along. Within the pyramid structure of feudalism, with kings and queens at the top and a descending hierarchy of dukes, earls, lords, knights, and peasants, everyone was slotted into their place. There was no flexibility, no social mobility, no room for innovation or individualism.

By smashing down this rigid social order, capitalism allowed people with talent, culture, and capital to break through. The wealthiest merchants and entrepreneurs began to emerge as the new ruling class in most countries, with the kings and queens and hereditary aristocrats swept aside – though in England and Scotland a compromise was reached, and the remnants of feudalism were allowed to remain in place.

The victory of the forces of capitalism over the forces of feudalism paved the way for an explosion in commerce and industry. Production of cotton, coal, iron, and a host of other commodities multiplied ten-fold. A vast network of roads, railways, and canals was constructed to transport the goods being churned out of the factories. Almost overnight, villages turned into towns and towns turned into cities. In every sphere of society – agriculture, industry, philosophy, politics, economics, religion, culture – it was a case of 'out with the old, in with the new'. For a time, capitalism was a truly revolutionary system and succeeded in transforming society from top to bottom.

But that was then and this is now. Technological progress continues, and will continue to continue *ad infinitum*. But capitalism has turned into a gigantic obstacle blocking the advance of civilisation. Far from being a vehicle for human progress, the profit system, more than ever before, retards, distorts, corrupts and stifles science.

At a time when the Internet revolution is turning the world of communications upside down, such an assertion might appear heretical. A decade ago, the World Wide Web did not even exist.

In 1992, there were just 100 websites. Today, there are hundreds of millions. Every day, it seems, exciting new innovations are reported. How can anyone seriously suggest that capitalism is holding back the forward march of history?

But even under feudalism, decisive technological advances took place. The first Information Revolution took place in the 15th century, with the invention of printing. This took place not because of feudalism, but despite feudalism. Indeed, the printed word was to become a revolutionary instrument in the hands of those fighting to overthrow feudalism. In France, for example, the publishing industry had exploded in the decades before the French Revolution in 1789. Over the previous century, the male literacy rate had doubled to 50 per cent and the female rate to 25 per cent. There was a proliferation of books and periodicals and by the 1790s it was estimated that one in four French adults were reading the revolutionary press.[1]

The Internet was not invented by businessmen and accountants. Nor, contrary to popular mythology, was it the brainchild of the US military. The US Defence Department only began to fund further research after they discovered that this was a communications network capable of surviving a nuclear war. But the network was actually developed in the first place by university-based computer scientists working, not in competition, but in collaboration with one another. It was not devised to make money; it was designed as a means of sharing information and knowledge.

The private sector only started to sit up and take notice in the mid-1990s after the technology, the software, and the pro-tocol system had already been thoroughly developed. According to Professor Douglas Rushkoff, a New York-based expert on communications technology, there has not been a single genuine innovation since big business took over.[2]

Recently an in-house variation on the light-bulb riddle has

been circulating among Microsoft employees. The question: how many Microsoft technicians does it take to change a light bulb? The answer: four. One to take the old one out. A second to rewire the socket so that only light bulbs produced by Microsoft will fit. A third to make sure that when the switch is flicked on, nothing happens. And a fourth to convince the government that Microsoft doesn't have a monopoly over the socket.

Every innovation by Microsoft and other software and hardware companies is designed for one purpose – to make more money. So what's the problem with that? Surely, if they are all competing with one another, they'll provide better faster cheaper easier-to-use computers, programs, and operating systems? In theory, that's what should happen, because that's what the free-market textbooks say should happen. But in the real world of cut-throat, greed-driven commerce, that's exactly what doesn't happen.

Instead software writers employed by computer manufacturers write programs that are designed to work only on the newest, fastest, most powerful computers. The aim is not to provide better software, but to force people to keep buying newer, faster, and more powerful computers to keep up. It's like buying a new brand of soap powder that washes your clothes cleaner, brighter, and whiter than any other soap powder. The only problem is, it won't work in your old washing machine, so you have to buy a new one.

New versions of programs are deliberately designed to be incompatible with the older versions of the same program. This causes communications problems and it forces consumers into an endless cycle of upgrades. But it makes money for big business, which is what capitalism is all about.

It is through co-operation rather than competition that the Internet was able to develop. All of the key advances – Eudora,

Usenet, the web browser, chat rooms – were designed in universities rather than in the research laboratories of private companies. Nor were these advances in information sold for profit. Instead, they were distributed free as 'shareware' – programs that anyone can download free of charge. Now a new operating system Linux, which is hailed by experts as by far superior to anything ever developed by Microsoft or Apple Mac, has arrived. It was designed by a student, who distributes the system free of charge to anyone who wants it.

We are repeatedly told that, without the profit motive, society would stagnate. Humans have an inborn desire to become richer than everyone else. This striving for wealth drives people to scale the heights of human knowledge and endeavour. And that's why we no longer live in caves cooking over open fires.

This is not just a fringe theory, like faith in reincarnation or yogic flying. This is the universally accepted, mainstream explanation of historical progress. It is the philosophy that underpins the entire economic and political system we live under. Yet, as a theory, it's as watertight as Rab C Nesbitt's string vest.

No significant scientific, medical, or cultural breakthrough in history has ever been inspired by greed. In general, the driving force of progress has been the natural human impulse to expand the horizons of human knowledge.

One of the world's greatest-ever inventors was Thomas Edison, who combined theoretical science with practical engineering. Edison established the Edison Electric Light Company, which later became General Electric, today one of the largest and most powerful transnational corporations on the planet. But Edison was interested in making things, not money. He recruited 20 of the top scientific brains in America, including mathematicians, physicists, engineers, chemists, and clockmakers to his institute, which was, in essence, the first-ever industrial laboratory. He and his colleagues invented, designed, and manufactured a whole array of products, including the first electric light bulb, the first electric train, and the first phonograph. They opened the door to the age of electricity and began to develop the rudiments of electronics, paving the way for radio, TV, and computers. But profit was not part of the calculation of these brilliant scientists. Edison himself denounced wealth and lived a modest and frugal lifestyle.[3]

Albert Einstein was the most brilliant scientist of the 20th century. Like Edison, he had no interest in riches. Early in his career, he decided to live a Spartan lifestyle. He reduced his personal requirements to the bare essentials – clothing, plain food, a modest house, no extravagant luxuries. His reasoning was that the pursuit of money and material comforts could distract him from his mission to push forward the frontiers of scientific knowledge. Einstein even wrote a pamphlet opposing capitalism, *Why Socialism?*[4]

John Logie Baird, living in poverty in an attic room, created the prototype television using makeshift materials such as a biscuit tin and cheap cycle lamps held together by darning needles and pieces of string. Louis Pasteur, Alexander Fleming, Alexander Graham Bell, and the other great innovators were similarly single-minded in their pursuit of knowledge and understanding.

One of the most hyped scientific breakthroughs of recent times has been the deciphering of the human genetic code. Genetic scientists estimate that up to 4000 hereditary diseases could eventually be eradicated or cured as a result of this breakthrough.

Yet no scientific advance illuminates more clearly the irreconcilable conflict between private greed and human progress. From 1990 onwards, the Human Genome Project in America and the Sanger Centre in Britain, both funded from charities and taxes, worked flat out to crack the so-called 'code of life'. Only after eight years of groundwork had been laid by public-sector scientists and researchers did the profiteers muscle in, scenting the possibility of piling up vast fortunes by patenting genetic information.

Here we have two diametrically opposed value systems. On the one side are the get-rich-quick merchants, whose aim is to make money. On the other side are dedicated scientists, who want to deepen understanding of the human make-up in order to assist the fight against cancer, diabetes, and AIDS.

The private profiteers hoard knowledge like dogs guarding their bones. If their capitalist value systems were to prevail in the field of genetic research, big business would control human evolution itself. Investigating remedies for baldness and wrinkles would become 1000 times more important than research into Third World diseases because they would be potentially 1000 times more profitable. Health services everywhere would be under the thumb of the venture capitalists.

But while the corporate mercenaries strike at the heart of scientific advance by treating information as a commodity to be bought and sold for profit, most of the world's great scientists operate by a different moral code. The Sanger Centre – which for a decade has spearheaded research into the genetic code – publishes all data free of charge on the Internet. Its director, Dr John Sulston, an avowed socialist, has no time for those who seek to profit from science. 'I don't want my genetic information to be under the control of any one entity or corporation,' he told *New Scientist* magazine.[5]

Similarly, most of the world's great writers, artists, and composers have been motivated by art rather than money. The life of Beethoven, for example, was one long struggle with poverty and debt. Instead of making himself rich by composing pretty tunes for the nobility, he composed music which was denounced as subversive by the reactionary rulers of his native Vienna. 'Words are in chains, but they can never silence my music,' the composer declared in defiance of the despots.

As a rule, it is whenever great artists sell out their talents to concentrate on making money that the standard of their art, literature, or music diminishes. But under capitalism, most gifted people come under pressure from the start to sell their talents to the highest bidder, invariably a big-business empire.

How many of the world's greatest scientists today are employed in the armaments industry, applying their genius to the grisly task of devising ever more murderous instruments of death and destruction? The American government spends $370 billion every year on defence, even though the US has never been invaded in its history. It spends 0.75 per cent of that figure – $2.5 billion – on research into cancer.[6]

The architect of the NHS, Nye Bevan, once said, 'Socialism is the language of priorities.' Under a socialist economic system, today's priorities would be turned upside down and inside out. Instead of devising laser-guided bombs that can be guided around street corners hundreds of miles distant, scientists and technicians could be employed to discover the causes of cancer and other deadly diseases, or to develop new forms of energy which do not harm the planet, or to devise ways of controlling the climate to prevent floods, droughts, and hurricanes, or to develop space travel and the exploration of the universe.

In the meantime, the advance of technology, warped and distorted though it has been up till now, is a deadly threat to the stability of capitalism.

According to the old adage, 'information is power'. In every society that has existed up till now, information has been under the control of a powerful elite. Everyone can buy a newspaper to find out what's happening in the world, or switch on the radio or TV news. But, as a general rule, the media are either under the control of rich businessmen or under the thumb of state governments. In theory, anyone can launch their own newspaper. There do exist today a few newspapers which do provide an alternative anti-Establishment slant. But these are run on a shoestring and cannot hope to compete with with the big-business-owned press.

Only the seriously rich possess the capital to produce a high-quality daily newspaper which requires printing presses, sophisticated equipment, and a small army of journalists, layout artists, photographers, accountants, receptionists, cashiers, van drivers, and other employees. It also requires access to the distribution network, which is controlled by a few big companies such as John Menzies in Scotland. In addition, newspapers and magazines are reliant on advertising revenues, which in turn shapes the content and political slant of the publication.

The Internet, by contrast, is open to everyone. Big business sees the Internet as a saviour. It is a means of by-passing national governments and avoiding restrictions on business imposed by national governments. Its vision of the Internet is of a vast singing, dancing marketplace, a global advertising bazaar geared solely towards commerce. But the reality is radically different. If you key the word 'Nike' or 'McDonald' into a search engine, it will call up the company's official websites. But it will also call up a host of other unofficial sites which provide the type of counter-information that the giant corporations would rather keep secret.

Usenet, the international network of mailing lists and newsgroups, has become the 21st-century version of the Roman Open Forum, where theories, ideologies, polemics, and masses of information are exchanged 24 hours a day.

The Internet has become the first international bastion of free speech and free thought. It is transforming the balance of forces between the powerful and the powerless. Without the Internet, the Mexican government would long ago have militarily crushed the Zapatistas. But this guerrilla movement, based deep in the jungles of Chiapas, has utilised the Internet to build around it a worldwide supporting cast of millions.

Ian Pearson, who is employed by BT as a 'futurologist', makes the point, 'Imagine re-running the feminist or environmental battles of the past few decades in an age when 98 per cent of the population are connected to the Internet. The economic muscle of the movement could be mobilised instantly and co-ordinated perfectly to much more rapid effect.'[7]

No sooner were these words written at the end of 1999 than they were spectacularly corroborated in the form of giant protests in Seattle and Washington against global capitalism. These protests were organised essentially via the World Wide Web. At the Washington demo, there was even a 'protest cam' that allowed people all over the world to view the events in real time on the Internet.

Interestingly, Pearson, in *Our View of the Future*, a series of documents published by BT to celebrate the new millennium, warns that capitalism cannot survive the advance of technology. 'The traditional capitalist system has worked very well to increase local, national, and global wealth for many years. However, it may have peaked already and, if not, the peak may arrive soon.'[8]

National governments are terrified by the disruptive potential of this free flow of information over cyberspace. But the horse has already bolted. It is true that governments can close down websites that they do not like. But human ingenuity has devised so many ways around cyber-censorship that it has become impossible to suppress information, short of closing down the entire telecommunications network.

Just as the printing revolution hastened the fall of feudalism by opening up a world of new ideas, so this new information revolution is likely to accelerate the drive to replace global capitalism with global socialism. Information has always been jealously guarded by the privileged elite who control society. But knowledge is rapidly being democratised by technology.

The advance of technology undermines two of the key arguments that have traditionally been deployed against socialism. The first of these is that socialism will lead to totalitarianism. This fear is one of the poisonous legacies of Stalinism. As we argue in more depth elsewhere in this book, totalitarianism was a product of conditions that do not apply in Scotland or anywhere else in Western Europe in the 21st century. Moreover, as Tony Benn once pointed out, blaming Karl Marx for the crimes of Stalinism is like blaming Jesus Christ for the Spanish Inquisition.

Nonetheless, the rise of communications technology should lay to rest any lingering fear that 'things could go wrong', that we could defeat capitalism only to have some tinpot dictator step in and take over. An essential precondition for totalitarianism is mass ignorance. Every totalitarian state in history has relied upon thought control. Only when people are kept in the dark can they be controlled.

Far from turning into an Orwellian nightmare, the triumph of hi-tech socialism could usher in the most democratic political system ever known. Instead of an elite group of middle-class politicians taking all the key political decisions, and another group of mega-rich businessmen taking all the key economic decisions, a genuine participatory democracy could be built.

At local, regional, national, and eventually international level, electronic voting, electronic consultation, and electronic referenda could bring about the most sweeping, democratic revolution in the history of the world. The fusion of a new egalitarian sociology with cutting-edge technology could allow direct democracy to flourish for the first time since ancient tribal society.

Chapter Eight

GREY SUITS AND GREEN RESISTANCE

BEFORE HIS DEATH a few years ago, the maverick financial tycoon, James Goldsmith, was one of the wealthiest men on the planet. He lived a lifestyle which few people could even begin to imagine.

But in the final years of his life he began to worry about the threat of global warming. The more knowledge he accumulated, the more anxious he became. Writing to his brother Teddy, he said, 'I feel like a man with a winning hand at poker . . . on the final night of the Titanic.'

The rich can escape most of the problems caused by capitalism. They never suffer hunger or homelessness. Their children are never taught in dilapidated overcrowded schools. They can shelter from crime by employing security staff and building the modern equivalent of the castle moat, the alarmed perimeter security fence. They can prolong their lives by buying access to the best medical care. Some genetic scientists have even predicted that, by the end of this century, the rich will be able to buy eternal life. But there is no hiding place, even for the Bill Gates and Rupert Murdochs, when the planet itself is threatened with extinction.

Yet, with the exception of individual mavericks like Goldsmith, the attitude of most big businessmen can be summed up in the phrase coined by the economist John Maynard Keynes, 'In the long run we'll all be dead.' They might well add, 'So in the short run we'll just pile up as much profit as we can, even if that means destroying natural habitats, depleting the earth's resources, and poisoning the air, the land, the seas.'

Bill Shankly, the famous football manager, was once asked in an interview if he believed that football was a matter of life and death. Jokingly, he replied, 'No – it's more important than that.' The threat to the global environment really is more than just a matter of life and death. It is potentially about the extinction of the human species after millions of years of evolution.

'But is this not just scaremongering by eco-warriors and naïve dreamers who want to halt all human progress?' some people ask. That's exactly what the people who run this planet want us to believe. But the threat of environmental destruction is serious, deadly serious.

Already, the needle has shot up into the red danger zone. Every second that ticks away, another ten acres of rainforest disappears. That's a lot of disappearing rainforest – over 300 million acres a year. Every six minutes another species becomes extinct – that's over 87,600 species wiped out every year. Every hour, almost seven square kilometres of fertile land is reduced to desert by global warming – that means every year a land area almost as large as Scotland becomes barren.[1]

Meanwhile the ocean floor is being systematically stripped of fish and other marine life by giant factory trawlers. The hole in the ozone layer continues to expand. The climate seems to be going haywire, with droughts and floods, typhoons and tornadoes, hurricanes and heatwaves, earthquakes and cyclones. As measured by average global temperature, 15 of the hottest years recorded have occurred in the past 20 years.[2]

Some of these changes may not appear at first glance to be all that important. Why should we be concerned about the fate of insects in the far away Amazon jungle? And even if the climate *is* changing, does it really matter?

The answer is, unfortunately, yes – it does really matter. Some time in the future, we may discover life on a distant planet. But we will never discover the exact life forms that exist on Earth. The way in which the species that inhabit our planet have evolved is a product of billions of interconnections. The human race itself could not have evolved separately and apart from the ecological system that surrounds us.

Just as the engine of a car is a finely-tuned combination of hundreds of parts, each of which relies upon the others to function, so the natural environment is a complex mixture of billions of related organisms. If the balance is repeatedly disturbed, the entire system can be thrown into disarray. As ecologists used to point out, under certain conditions the flap of a butterfly's wings can trigger off an avalanche.

No-one knows the precise long-term effects of environmental desecration, or the exact speed at which the destruction of our planet is proceeding. Some scientists, including those at the Hadley Centre, which is linked to the UK Met Office, warn that within 50 years, the Earth could face disturbances so severe that the future of the planet could be called into question.[3] Some of the less apocalyptic predictions include huge disruption of agriculture, the collapse of national economies, and the creation of millions of environmental refugees, as the sea submerges nations such as Bangladesh and turns other nations into vast deserts.

Others fear that human economic activity has already set in motion forces which are spiralling out of control. At a certain point, warns Peter Bunyard in *The Ecologist*, there could be runaway global warming with incalculable consequences for the future of the planet.[4]

For some environmentalists, the only solution is to halt all economic development. Others go even further and promote a 'back to the land' lifestyle and a return to a pre-industrial rural utopia, which as it happens, never existed outside the imagination of the authors of romantic historical novels. Before large-scale industry blighted the landscape, life was short and consisted of physical drudgery without end.

It is no more possible to turn back the calendar to an earlier economic age than it is to force the River Clyde to flow backwards. There are more people living on the planet today than there are people who have died throughout the whole of human history. And of the six billion inhabitants of our planet, at least three billion live in conditions of extreme poverty. Without large-scale industry, life on planet Earth would descend into barbarism.

But one thing is more clear than ever before: human progress cannot be a free-for-all. It has to be consciously planned and monitored. Manic haphazard economic growth, driven by the demands of shareholders for bigger and faster profits, is threatening the future of civilisation. The road to hell is paved with corporate balance sheets.

Every minute of every day, industry churns out mountains of cheap useless tacky goods, designed to instantly fall apart or stop working. Light bulbs, batteries, cigarette lighters, and a multitude of other products on the market are guaranteed to have a short lifespan, because if they had a long lifespan, demand for these products would collapse, and so would the profits of the companies that produce them.

Colossal amounts of time, resources, and physical and mental effort are devoted to inventing, developing, producing, marketing, and selling things that no-one really needs. In the 1970s sitcom, *The Fall and Rise of Reginald Perrin*, the main character opened a chain of 'Grot Shops', selling totally useless items at ridiculously high prices. Incredibly, 1970s satire has become 21st-century reality. For example, it's possible to buy a variety of different walking boots, cotton-fleece sweaters, quilted jackets, and electric blankets – for your dog or cat! One commercially successful website is devoted exclusively to selling bizarre items such as nose-shaped pencil sharpeners, Spam-flavoured bubble gum, and a lollipop that doubles up as a fire extinguisher.

Through high-powered advertising, an artificial demand is created. One socialist economist pointed to the bizarre example of the funeral industry in America, which successfully marketed coffins with foam mattresses to keep corpses comfortable.[5]

Under a socialist economy, wasteful production could be reduced to a minimum. In some areas of the economy, increased production will be necessary. For example, where there is a problem of homelessness and sub-standard housing, one of the immediate priorities of any socialist government would be to employ construction workers to build houses. There will be a need, too, for a big expansion of public transport, which could involve excavating metros, laying down rail tracks, manufacturing trains, buses, minibuses, and ferries.

Agricultural production also needs to be increased on an international scale to wipe out starvation in the Third World. Back in the 1980s, Tracy Chapman sang, 'How can a baby starve, when there's enough food to feed the world?' In the strictest technical sense, that may be the case. But, as the environmental writer, Susan George, points out in her book, *The Lugano Report*, this would mean the entire population of the world switching to exactly the same vegetarian diet of grains and pulses and an end to the production of such 'luxury' items as wine, beer, and various fruits and oils. Even then, there would still be nutritional deficiencies: for example, someone whose work consists of heavy manual labour needs 4500 calories a day, yet the maximum that could be provided with present harvests is 2300 calories per head.[6]

The giant biotechnology companies like Monsanto, AgrEvo and Norvartis proclaim genetically modified foods as the answer to starvation. Yet tests conducted so far show that biologically modified plants release toxins which can multiply and spread right across the food chain via spores and insects, with potentially nightmarish consequences for the whole of human, animal, plant, and insect life. The real aim of companies such as Monsanto is not to feed the Third World but to feed the greed of their own shareholders. Their ultimate aim is to wipe out traditional farming and grab control of the world's food supply.

Socialists do not oppose scientific progress. But a whole series of catastrophes and cover-ups, from the Three Mile Island nuclear explosion to the Thalidomide scandal, have taught us that science under the control of big business can never be trusted.

Nothing short of a new agrarian revolution to oust the giant landowners and re-establish food production on a co-operative basis worldwide will be required to end starvation. But other areas of production could be scaled down, or even stopped completely, under socialism. In a future worldwide confederation of socialist states there would be no need for armaments production. With millions of nicotine addicts in the world today, it may take a generation or two to halt cigarette production, but it is likely that some time before the end of this century, dangerous drugs such as tobacco will be available only on prescription.

Wasteful production of luxury goods for the rich could be halted. Over the past decade there has been a global spending spree on executive jets, luxury yachts, private helicopters, mink coats, Rolls-Royces, and a whole array of items that devour resources, time, and labour, purely for the purpose of enhancing the prestige of the rich.

At the other end of the scale, quality-control systems would be introduced to stop the flooding of the world's markets with cheap trashy goods, which generally end up in the rubbish bin within days of purchase.

The production of plastics, polystyrene, synthetic fibres, and other chemical products that pollute the atmosphere would be scaled down to a minimum, in favour of natural products. Wasteful production on packaging, junk mail, and the like would be strictly regulated, while recycling would become one of the big growth industries in a new socialised economy.

Today in the USA alone, 50 per cent of all paper and 90 per cent of all glass is used for packaging. A 1992 survey conducted in Britain found that of the average £75 supermarket shopping bill, £10 goes towards the cost of packaging.

A harmoniously planned socialist economy could also phase out fossil fuels – the biggest single cause of global warming – and move towards new forms of energy, including wind, wave, and solar power. In California, wind farms already supply the equivalent of San Francisco's entire domestic power consumption.

The sun is an even more powerful generator of energy. Contrary to popular belief, it's not necessary to have a Mediterranean climate before solar power can be harnessed. Just 15 minutes of sunshine has the potential to generate more energy than the world consumes in a year, and even Scotland enjoys the odd quarter of an hour of sunshine now and again. The sun could provide clean, safe energy for another billion years. Yet, right now, because no-one anywhere is putting serious money into researching and developing it, solar power only generates 0.001 per cent of the world's energy.

This may seem a rather strange oversight on the part of the world's economic and political leaders. Every day, new reports provide fresh evidence of galloping global warming, increasing pollution, and rising rates of bronchial disease due to noxious fumes. Surely it's in everyone's interests to change course?

Unfortunately, it's not in everyone's interests. There are indescribably powerful vested interests opposing the development of new sources of clean, safe, and sustainable energy. The fossil-fuel industries, for example, are worth one trillion dollars a year. And even capitalism has not yet devised a way of privatising the wind, or of floating the sun on the stock exchange, or of selling the sea off to the highest bidder.

Companies like BP-Amoco are part of the Global Climate Coalition, a benevolent-sounding organisation, which actually promotes global warming by campaigning against restrictions on fuel pollution. The GCC employs scientists on sky-high salaries to create a veneer of objectivity, and spin doctors on similarly inflated salaries to misinform and mislead the public.

The big oil and vehicle-manufacturing companies will move Heaven and Earth to protect their profits and investments. Some years ago, General Motors, Standard Oil, and the Firestone Tyre Company actually conspired to destroy electric-rail transport systems in 45 American cities. General Motors bought over the systems, ripped up the tracks, and replaced the electric trains with buses as a way of forcing the government to construct new roads.[8]

Some environmentalists like to stand above the murky old politics of class, capitalism, and socialism. 'Neither Left nor Right but Green' is their motto. This attitude is partly a backlash against the Stalinist model of bureaucratic centralism pursued in the Soviet Union and Eastern Europe. These states vandalised the natural environment with the same reckless abandon with which transnational capitalism desecrates the planet. Events like Chernobyl caused appalling devastation way beyond the borders of the Soviet Union itself. But rejecting socialism because of the appalling track record of Stalinism is like refusing to eat mushrooms because toadstools are poisonous.

The battle between socialism and capitalism is essentially a conflict over whether the resources of the planet should be owned and controlled by a wealthy minority, or by the people of the planet. The radical environmentalist who refuses to take sides in that struggle between Left and Right is like the condemned man who refuses to take sides in the argument over capital punishment.

Inevitably, there will be big debates within the socialist movement and in a future socialist society over environmental questions. There will be conflict between those who want to emphasise conservation and those who want to emphasise sustainable economic development. There will be disputes over the *pace* of change, for example, from traditional fossil fuels to alternative forms of energy. There will be wide-ranging discussions on how best to protect the planet's resources while prosecuting the war against poverty and want. There will be all sorts of disputes on all sorts of issues at local, national, and international level.

But without democratic ownership of land, industry, transport, energy, and finance, there can be no real democratic control. Ultimately, the destiny of the planet is a political fight to transfer ownership of the planet from the billionaires to the billions.

No way does that mean environmentalists should stop fighting back against road-building projects, or against toxic-waste dumps, or against opencast mines, or against nuclear power. One of the best slogans of the environmental movement is 'Think global, act local'. But the struggle to save the planet is more than just a series of unconnected battles to stop this road, to save this natural habitat, or to close down this poisonous landfill site. We have to fight many individual battles, but we also have to win the war eventually.

Like the war against global poverty, the war against global environmental destruction has to begin at home. The building of a green socialist Scotland some time within the first few decades of this new century would not protect Scotland against the impact of global warming. Pollution knows no national boundaries – the east coast of the Republic of Ireland is as much affected by the radioactive poisons from the Sellafield nuclear-power plant as the west coast of England, Wales, or Scotland. Nonetheless, the defeat of capitalism by red-green forces in any country, even in a small country the size of Scotland, would represent a huge advance for the forces of socialism and radical environmentalism.

Most people from outside look at Scotland and imagine that it's some kind of environmental paradise. We live in one of the most sparsely populated countries in Europe, with vast wildernesses of moor and mountain, thousands of miles of coastline, thousands of islands, lochs, rivers, and a temperate climate.

But this small country is also home to most of Europe's nuclear weapons. Our seas to the north and east are ravaged for oil and gas by corporate pirates, who have now begun to explore the spectacular ocean wilderness surrounding St Kilda in the far north-west. Our seas to the south-west contain over a million tons of conventional and chemical weapons. Parts of the northern Highlands have been turned into dumping grounds for nuclear waste from all over the world.

Opencast mining is marauding across the central belt, turning huge tracts of picturesque countryside into ugly scars. Lorryloads of toxic waste from the Home Counties career through our towns and villages en route to toxic-waste dumps in Lanarkshire. Poisonous cocktails of deadly metals are being pumped into the Forth. There have been numerous radioactive leakages into the Firth of Forth from Rosyth, and into the Firth of Clyde from Faslane.

Under new ownership, under new management, we could turn Scotland into a clean green country, a living breathing example of socialist environmentalism in action. We could close down the Trident nuclear bases and use some of the savings to retrain and redeploy the entire Faslane and Coulport workforce. As Scottish CND has repeatedly pointed out, if the costs of Trident were redirected to other areas of the economy, for every one job lost, another five could be created.

We may not be able to make Dounereay completely safe; the damage has already been done. But we could make it a great deal safer than it is right now. We could also use some of the proceeds from North Sea oil to pioneer wind, wave, and even solar energy. We could seal off the pollutants that contaminate our seaways. We could close the toxic dumps and halt the desecration of our natural landscape by the opencast mining companies.

We could transform public transport. Politicians spout endlessly about the need to reduce car usage. But sometimes a ten-minute car journey can take up to an hour by bus. You've walked to the bus stop, you've waited for the bus to arrive, you've felt your blood pressure rising as the bus winds its way slowly through city streets, stopping for a couple of minutes every few hundred yards to pick up more passengers. The next time you just take the car.

In a socialist Scotland, investment would be ploughed into building a hi-tech, low-fare, super-efficient public-transport system. The exact shape of a radical new public-transport network could be worked out democratically, with communities, transport workers, environmental specialists, and local and national government all involved in drawing up plans for improving existing systems and initiating new projects.

The reopening of the rail network that used to criss-cross rural Scotland, the extension of the Glasgow Underground to the outlying housing schemes and the suburbs, the excavation of a new metro system in Edinburgh, the establishment of a system of on-call minibuses to take passengers to the nearest rail station or bus terminus; all of these measures and much, much more would be possible.

But not while we are at the mercy of privatised rail and bus companies whose sole aim is to maximise their own profits. Social ownership of the bus, rail, and ferry companies wouldn't automatically reduce car use or provide an overnight solution to all the transport problems we face. But it could be and should be the starting point for a transport revolution in Scotland.

An independent socialist Scotland could also instigate an agricultural revolution by banning genetically modified crops and foods and farm crops and subsidising our farmers to switch to organic production. There has been an explosive growth internationally in the demand for organic food. Tesco reported a 20-fold increase in sales of organic produce over three years; Sainsbury reported a 125-fold increase over four years. Yet 70 per cent of organic foods are imported, and are also expensive. Only 1.5 per cent of the total farmed land in Britain is devoted to organic agriculture. Yet only £6 million in aid has been made available in the last year to help farmers convert to organic methods.[9]

These changes are not outlandish fantasies. They are practical, they are sensible, they are rational. But even these moderate measures to restore the balance of nature and to protect the health and safety of the people of Scotland would require revolutionary changes in the way society is organised.

We could leave well alone, cross our fingers, and hope that the scientists, the ecologists, the meteorologists, the naturalists, the horticulturalists have got it all wrong and the businessmen have got it all right. Or we can resign ourselves to the fact that, yes, there is a problem, and with any luck somebody, somewhere, some time, will do something about it. But, as another slogan of the international green movement warns, 'Tomorrow may be too late.'

Chapter Nine

BLOOD, LAND AND OIL

IN HIS BOOK *Who Owns Scotland* Andy Wightman relates the story of a Fife miner walking home one evening, carrying some illegally poached pheasants. Suddenly, the local landowner appears at his side and demands he hand over the pheasants.

'Don't you know that this is my land and these are my pheasants?' brays the landowner.

'And where did you get it?' asks the miner.

'I inherited it from my father!' replies the landowner.

'So where did he get it?'

'From his father. This land has belonged to my family for 500 years.'

'And where did they get it from 500 years ago?'

'They fought for it.'

'Well, then,' says the miner. 'Take off your jacket and I'll fight you for it!'[1]

In *Our Scots Noble Families*, published back in 1909, Forward editor, Tom Johnston, lambasted the Scottish aristocracy. 'Our Nobility is not noble. Its lands are stolen lands – stolen either by force or fraud . . . the title deeds are rapine, murder, massacre, cheating or Court harlotry.'[2]

The old Scottish aristocracy has been partly squeezed out by a new breed of absentee landowners. Almost as much Scottish land is now held by overseas landowners as is held by the traditional aristocracy. Nonetheless, many of the same noble families that

Johnston pilloried at the beginning of last century continue to own vast expanses of rural Scotland. This self-perpetuating elite includes the Duke of Buccleuch, the Earl of Seafield, the Duke of Sutherland, the clan chieftain, Captain Alwyn Farqhuarson, and the Duke of Roxburghe. The 280,000 acres owned by the Duke of Buccleuch stretch all the way from the Firth of Forth to the Solway Firth.

Not so long ago, the 29th Chieftain of the MacLeod clan, John MacLeod of MacLeod decided to fix his leaky roof. Most people would have flicked through the *Yellow Pages* and called in the builders. If necessary, they'd maybe take out a bank loan to pay the bill. But, when you live in Dunvegan Castle, more grandiose measures are called for. The owner of the majestic fortress decided he needed £10 million to fix his roof, so he tried to put the entire Cuillin mountain range up for sale.

The Cuillin is one of the most dramatic landscapes in Northern Europe, a mountain wilderness covering 25 square miles of southern Skye. If someone tried to sell you the North Pole, or Mount Everest, or the Grand Canyon, you'd probably take pity on them. But in 21st-century Scotland, these types of transaction take place all the time. It's as though the last five centuries had never happened.

If anything, as time goes on, landownership in Scotland has become even more grotesquely concentrated in fewer and fewer hands. In no other country in Europe, nor even in Latin America, with its notorious economic disparities, is there such an unequal distribution of land.

According to Wightman's brilliantly researched book, 16 million of Scotland's 19 million acres of land are privately owned. Two thirds of this land is owned by 1252 landowners. Or, to put it another way, 0.025 per cent of the population owns 66 per cent of Scotland.[3]

Not just in Europe, but throughout most of the world, there

are restrictions on landownership. In most of Europe, no-one is allowed to buy land unless they intend to spend most of the year actually living on it. They also require to register their possession of land and have to submit to stringent regulations and conditions.

But not in Scotland. Here anyone can buy land. Then they can do what they want with that land. They can increase the rents for the tenants and small farmers who live on the land. They can leave it to rack and ruin. They can break it up into smaller packages and flog these off to stalking, shooting, and angling companies who then turn the land into playgrounds for the rich. They can erect signposts, as one landowner around Loch Cluny did, announcing that 'This mountain is closed.'

And they have immense power over the lives of the communities who live on their land. Lord Vestey, the meat-industry tycoon who owns the 100,000-acre Assynt estate has been described as 'the richest man in the Highlands'. This would be an accurate description if he actually lived in the Highlands. In fact, he lives in Suffolk and works in London.

Yet according to local people in Assynt, Vestey has stopped a swimming pool being built in an area that has a desperate lack of amenities, prevented a new housing development in a community with a dire housing shortage, and thwarted plans to establish a factory unit in a part of the Highlands that is being steadily depopulated because of lack of work.[4]

Before the people of Eigg took over ownership of the island, it had been owned by a Yorkshire millionaire, Keith Schellenberg, who denounced the entire population of the island as 'hippies and hooligans'. He then sold it on to a German painter, Marlin Maruma, who decided on a whim to buy the island, then visited it exactly twice in two years.

Few other countries in the world would allow vast tracts of land to be sold off to wealthy individuals for the purpose of indulging in an extravagant hobby. Yet, in Scotland, there are now 800 huge sporting estates, according to the British Association for Shooting and Conservation. These estates cost hundreds of thousands of pounds each to run.

The landowners claim that these estates create jobs. Yet as Auslan Cramb points out in his book *Who Owns Scotland Now?*, there are estates in the Highlands of 50,000 acres and more which employ just a handful of people on bare subsistence wages. The fact is, far more jobs could be created if these sporting estates were taken into public and community ownership and run democratically, in the interests of the local population.

There are reputedly some good landowners who co-operate with local communities and are conscious of the need to protect the environment. No doubt, in the Middle Ages, some feudal barons were more humanitarian than others in their treatment of the vassals they owned. Even some slave owners occasionally treated their slaves almost as generously as they treated their pets. But why, in the 21st century, should rural communities be forced to cross their fingers collectively and hope that the next wealthy landowner who comes along will be a benevolent paternalistic laird rather than a tinpot tyrant?

As Dutch land specialist, Jan van de Ploeg, from the Agricultural University at Wageningen, observed on the BBC TV programme, *Eorpa*, 'It is very curious how people treat land in Scotland. Land is simply a commodity. This is wild west capitalism. One of the most valuable assets for the future, the land, can be bought and sold at will. Elsewhere in Europe that is not the case. It makes Scotland a truly unique case.'[5]

There have been a few mild land reforms introduced by the Scottish Parliament since then, but the words of van de Ploeg are still 100 per cent relevant. Communities are now allowed to purchase land, but first they have to wait, perhaps for generations, before the land comes onto the market. Then they have to raise colossal sums of money to buy the land, not an easy feat for the average sparsely populated and impoverished community in an area like the West Highlands.

In *Who Owns Scotland Now?*, Auslan Cramb expresses some sympathy for the aristocratic Sutherland clan dynasty, who are still ostracised for the cold cruelty displayed by their ancestors during the Highland Clearances. 'The atrocities of Nazi Germany, much more recently, are not visited on decent Germans today,' protests Cramb.

But 'decent Germans today' did not inherit ownership of Germany from their Nazi ancestors. The Scottish aristocracy want to have their cake and eat it. They complain when they are snubbed from officiating at the Gaelic Mod because their ancestors set out to liquidate Gaelic culture. Yet they simultaneously claim a divine right to ownership of vast lands because they happen to have been born into the right family.

The priests in Latin America who preach Liberation Theology denounce private landownership as immoral. Their philosophy is simple: the land was created by God, therefore no human being has a right to claim personal ownership of that land. It is not necessary to subscribe to any religious belief to be in broad sympathy with that philosophy.

In a future socialist Scotland, the land will be legally recognised as the common property of the Scottish people. That doesn't mean that the state would seize people's houses and gardens, or collectivise small and medium-sized farms.

It does mean bringing sporting estates and other unoccupied land into social or community ownership under democratic local management. It does mean imposing upper limits on landholdings, which would vary depending on the quality and use of land. It does mean giving local communities the opportunity to leasehold land on a co-operative or communal basis and run the land themselves.

And it does mean dragging Scotland out of the 18th century and into the 21st century by ending the system that allows individuals to own vast empires of mountains and lochs, farms and crofts, towns and villages, all because of the blood that flows through their veins, or the cash that flows through their bank accounts.

Scotland may not be classified a Third World country, but like most of Africa, Asia, and Latin America, our natural resources are greedily grabbed up by whatever rich individual or powerful company comes along and writes a cheque. Only the rain that falls from the skies is still owned by the people of Scotland, and that's only because the people of Scotland refused to allow the last Tory government to sell it to the City spivs.

Unfortunately, the oil that lies underneath the North Sea has already been sold off, or, to be more precise, it has been given away. According to the SNP, 'It's Scotland's Oil.' New Labour say, 'No, it's Britain's oil.' As is usually the case, both sets of politicians are wrong. Britain doesn't own North Sea oil. Nor would Scotland own North Sea oil, even if the SNP were to take power in an independent Scotland.

The truth is, North Sea oil is owned, lock, stock, and barrel, by a collection of transnational oil companies. Not that these companies actually created the oil, any more than the feudal barons and clan chieftains created the land that their descendants now own. Nor did the oil companies even discover the oil in the first place.

It was first discovered in 1962 by the British government, who set out looking for gas and accidentally discovered black gold buried deep beneath the North Sea. By 1964, Whitehall had handed out 100,000 square miles of sea-bed to multinational oil companies for exploration. Since the oil began to flow in 1969, these companies have made hundreds of billions of pounds of profit for their shareholders. Scotland has received a fraction of that money.

In March 2000 oil revenues were running at almost £45 million a day, according to the Royal Bank of Scotland. Of that cash, around £13 million went to the British exchequer in corporation tax. Around £1.3 million of that was directed back to Scotland, as our share of UK revenues. Meanwhile, the oil companies grabbed over £30 million a day. In other words, every day, a few thousand North Sea oil-company shareholders receive 25 times more than the whole of Scotland with its five million inhabitants.[6]

In most other oil-producing countries in the world, such a state of affairs would be incomprehensible. In Malaysia, Brazil, Mexico, Venezuela, South Korea, and across the Middle East, oil is publicly owned. Some of these national governments have come under pressure from the International Monetary Fund to privatise the industry in order to raise instant cash to pay off national debts. Invariably, this has provoked the type of public backlash that the British Tory government faced when it tried to privatise Scottish water.

In a country like Mexico, the publicly owned oil company Pemex generates up to 40 per cent of all government revenues. In Norway, where the industry is now under threat of privatisation from a right-wing government, the largest oil company is fully publicly owned, while the two other oil companies are part publicly owned. As a result, the Norwegian government has been awash with money and has been able to carry out extensive social and welfare programmes.

In 1974, Britain elected a Labour government led by Harold Wilson, which promised to nationalise North Sea oil. In power, Wilson decided the policy was 'impractical'. But it wasn't impractical in Malaysia, which in 1974 took over the country's oilfields. Nor was it impractical in Venezuela, which followed suit two years later. Today, the publicly owned Malaysian oil corporation, Petronas, is included in the *Fortune 500* largest companies in the world; while the state-owned Petreolos de Venezuela is now the third biggest exporter of crude oil in the world.

The attitude of successive British governments was lampooned a quarter of a century ago in John McGrath's ground-breaking play, *The Cheviot, the Stag, and the Black, Black Oil*, performed by the newly formed 7:84 Theatre Company. In one scene, an American oil tycoon performs a frenzied barn dance, singing

'Take your oil-rigs by the score,
Drill a little well just a little off-shore,
Pipe that oil in from the sea,
Pipe those profits – home to me.'

He then tells the audience: 'Your wonderful Labourite government was real nice: thank God they weren't socialists.'

The 'Labourite' governments of the 1960s and 1970s certainly were not socialists. But today's 'Labourite government' is truly beyond satire. While Harold Wilson occasionally issued threats – albeit empty threats – of nationalisation to the oil companies, Tony Blair is flown out by BP to inaugurate the opening of the new Andrew Field, on which trade unions are to be refused recognition. He then goes on to appoint the BP chief executive, Lord Simon, to the post of Minister of Trade in the New Labour government.

One of Blair's Scottish allies, Martin O'Neill MP, calls for longer shifts for oil workers and for oil companies to be exempted from the European Union Social Chapter. Another, the ex-Shadow Secretary of State, George Robertson, now head of NATO, solemnly assured a gathering of oil bosses that Labour wanted 'to reduce costs for the oil companies'; in other words, to increase the profits of the oil moguls at the expense of wages and safety conditions.[7]

It is a bizarre fact that in the 30 years since North Sea oil began to flow ashore, the Shetland Islands council has put up more resistance to the oil transnationals than the entire procession of Labour-Tory-Labour-Tory-Labour governments combined. Shetland imposed a local tax of 15 pence on every barrel passing through and insisted on a guaranteed annual payment of at least £750,000 for local services. In a rather bizarre outburst, the man who in the 1970s was the United States consul in Scotland, representing the world's mightiest superpower in the 1970s, later described tiny Shetland as 'the tyrant that bestrode oil'.[8]

While the savage Shetlanders tyrannised the poor defenceless oil companies, successive British governments were far more reasonable. They abolished petroleum revenue tax. They refused to take royalties. They slashed corporation tax to just 30 per cent, the lowest rate by far of any major country in Europe. They allowed the oil giants to ban trade unions. They let the oil companies away with murder – literally, claim some of the relatives of the 167 workers killed in the Piper Alpha explosion in 1988.

Like the Tories before them, the New Labour government believes that nothing must be allowed to stand in the way of free enterprise. Unfortunately, the SNP has an even more subservient attitude. They want to cut corporation tax even further, possibly to less than half of its current level.

Most mainstream politicians these days have resigned themselves to market forces. 'We live in a global economy,' they say. 'And in a global economy you can't buck market forces.' Nor can you bring industries into social ownership, because that's against the rules of global capitalism. That would be piracy. And, in any case, we haven't got the expertise to run an industry as complex as the oil industry. And, by the way, don't you realise that big business can simply pull out and relocate to the other side of the world these days if it doesn't like what you're doing?

All these arguments can be distilled down to a single word:

baloney. If a whole series of countries managed to take over and successfully run their own oil industry back in the 1970s, how come we don't have the expertise today, when Aberdeen is the oil capital of Europe and Scotland has been producing oil for over 30 years?

And how is it possible to relocate an oilfield anyway? The Internet may be a powerful new tool, but no-one has yet developed the technology that can spirit away 100 oilfields to the other side of the world via modems and broad-band cables.

New Labour and the Tories repeatedly insist that an independent Scotland would be uneconomic, that it would have a deficit of billions. But an independent Scotland that owned and controlled the revenues flooding in from North Sea oil would have a surplus of anything between £10 billion to £15 billion a year, depending upon fluctuations in world oil prices.

It would allow for the greatest expansion of public services that this country has ever seen. And it would also generate the resources to allow an independent socialist Scotland to face up to one of the biggest challenges of the 21st century, the building of a brand-new energy industry based on alternative, renewable sources of power.

The Cheviot, the Stag, and the Black, Black Oil ended with a Gaelic song written in the 1890s by Mary MacPherson, whose family was driven from the Isle of Skye during the Highland Clearances. In English, the song says:

> 'Remember your hardships and keep up your struggle,
> The wheel will turn for you,
> By the strength of your hands and hardness of your fists.
> Your cattle will be on the plains,
> Everyone in the land will have a place,
> And the exploiter will be driven out.'

The exploiter still has not been driven out. Back in the days when he was a socialist, Gordon Brown condemned the SNP for their acceptance of the private ownership of land, oil, and other industries, and for their rejection of class politics: 'The SNP's "new politics", which rejects "class warfare", presumes the familiar priorities of wealth and power over people ... Their rejection of public ownership of land, oil, and the basic industries ... assumes the subservience of Scottish workers to private international controls.' [9]

Now, as Chancellor of the Exchequer, the same Gordon Brown resists pressure for a paltry penny-in-the-pound increase in corporation tax for the oil companies, even though, as the *Petroleum Economist* magazine notes approvingly, 'The UK's tax system for oil and gas ventures is the most attractive of any established producing country worldwide.'[10]

The Gordon Brown who sits in Downing Street today may have grown 25 years older, and 25 times richer, sleeker, and more conservative, but the exploiters are still exploiting Scotland's natural resources for private greed. Eventually, as Mary MacPherson said, they will be driven out.

Chapter Ten

TYRANNY OF THE BALANCE SHEET

AS YOU READ this, you may well be sipping a mug of tea. On the face of it, tea is one of the simplest drinks on the market. Unlike most soft drinks, for example, it's made from a few basic natural ingredients.

A few tea leaves, perhaps crushed up and wrapped inside a paper tea bag, some boiling water, and that's it. Simple to produce, you might imagine. But is it? What processes are involved in delivering that tea into your cup?

In the first place, tea-plantation workers in Sri Lanka, India, or Bangladesh farm and collect the tea leaves which are then packaged up, transported to the nearest docks, and loaded onto a cargo ship. The tea is then shipped halfway round the world and unloaded by another group of dockers onto lorries. From the port, the raw tea is then transported by road to a processing factory, where it's turned into the tea bag that you drop into your mug or teapot. It's also packed into brightly labelled boxes, made in a separate factory. The boxes are produced by printers and designers, by paper-mill workers, and by foresters who cut down the trees which supply the paper mills.

The boxes of tea bags are then transported to supermarkets and corner shops all over the UK. Without oil workers and petrochemical refinery workers you wouldn't be sitting right now enjoying a cup of tea. The lorries themselves, and the ships too, which transport the tea across the world to your local super-market, consist of thousands of separate components all produced in factories by workers from hundreds of different trades.

In other words, a vast network of people – from tea plantation farmers to dockers, from shipyard workers to shop assistants, from lumberjacks to oil workers – are involved in delivering that tea bag into your cup. And almost every product on sale in your local Asda or Tesco superstore involves a similarly complex process of collaboration across industries, countries and continents.

Back in the mists of history, production was much simpler. It involved individuals, or small groups of individuals, making some items and exchanging these items for other items. In today's ultra-sophisticated economy, production is carried out socially and collectively rather than privately and individually. It involves a phenomenal amount of collaboration and co-ordination.

Yet each link in the chain of production is controlled by private individuals and run for their own self-interest and that of their shareholders. Production and distribution is carried out socially but all of the instruments of production and distribution – computer systems, transport systems, superstores, factories, offices, machines, vehicles, power stations, telephone cables – are owned by private individuals.

Without co-operation no modern society could function. But co-operation in a profit-based economy is subverted at each stage by the competing pressures and demands of rival capitalists who try to rip off each other, rip off the customer, rip off their workforces. Under capitalism we have a patchwork quilt of rival business empires each accountable only to its own shareholders, and each run purely for profit. If something can be produced for profit, it will be produced, no matter how useless, wasteful, or destructive that product is. But if something *can't* be produced for profit it *won't* be produced at all, no matter how desperately that product is needed.

Back in the middle of the 19th century, life expectancy in the city of Glasgow was 30 years. Deadly diseases such as cholera and typhoid rampaged through the city's tenements, wiping out thousands at a time in epidemics.

Then, in 1859, a spectacularly ambitious and far-sighted project was launched with the aim of transporting water to Glasgow from Loch Katrine. In a remarkable feat of engineering, an elaborate network of pipes and viaducts was constructed across a 35-mile stretch of mountainous countryside. When the water began to flow through the taps, there was a miraculous improvement in sanitation and health in the most overcrowded and disease-ridden city in northern Europe.[1]

While all this was taking place, private enterprise was nowhere to be seen. This was a public enterprise, spearheaded by the municipal council. Its aim was not to make profits for share-holders, but to extend the lifespan of ordinary people.

The tobacco industry by contrast, shortens the life of ordinary people. It kills more people every year than are killed in wars. Five big tobacco giants alone employ over 500,000 people across the globe to manufacture billions of cigarettes. Each of these cigarettes contains at least 4000 chemicals, of which 42 have been proved to cause cancer.[2]

If a fraction of the resources that are dedicated to producing, advertising, and distributing cigarettes were devoted instead to research into cancer, the disease would now be history. In Britain, £150 million a year is spent in cancer research – barely one per cent of the total amount spent on tobacco. Meanwhile the tobacco companies slaughter more and more people every year. Last year three million people died from diseases caused by smoking. According to the World Health Organisation, that figure will rise to 10 million within 20 years as the tobacco corporations seek to expand their market by creating millions more nicotine addicts in the Third World.

Even more colossal than the tobacco industry is the armaments industry. In Europe and the US alone, £400 billion a year is spent on arms. In Britain, around 500,000 people are employed directly or indirectly in manufacturing weapons which will be used to kill people. The whole industry drains talent, time, energy, materials, and money.

The UK government has just signed a contract to buy 232 Eurofighter planes. Each of these planes will cost £39 million. Their total cost – £9 billion – is double the total annual spending on the NHS in Scotland.[3] The companies that build these planes could easily switch to producing different products. They could manufacture kidney dialysis machines, scanners, or incubators for our hospitals. They could build hi-tech light-railway systems to relieve the congestion on our roads. They could provide electricity-powered mobile wheelchairs for everyone who needed such a vehicle. But they won't, because there is no profitable market for these things.

The tobacco and defence industries are dramatic examples of production for destruction. The advertising industry, by contrast, does not slaughter people physically. Nor is there anything wrong, in principle, with advertising. Every organisation, whether it be a charity, a business, a political party, a campaigning body, or a government institution uses advertising in one form or another to convey information to the public. Advertising can even benefit the public, up to a point, by providing information. If you want to know which films are showing at your local cinema, you buy an evening newspaper and look at the advertisements. Some charity and campaign adverts can even be informative.

But the industry as a whole has turned into an insatiable devourer of talent and resources. There are now 200,000 people in America and 50,000 people in the UK employed in public relations. Every year, an estimated £1000 billion is spent on advertising and marketing.[4]

Pharmaceutical companies, for example, spend twice as much on advertising as they do on research. During the winter, these companies bombard us with adverts for cold and flu remedies. High Street chemists display a dazzling array of powders and pills, in brightly coloured packages. Each one claims to have greater magical powers than the rest. In fact, they all contain exactly the same basic ingredients. It's easy to be misled into thinking that this bewildering assortment of rival brands represents some kind of choice. In reality, they are essentially the same products in different packets. Often, they are produced in the same factories, as are other kinds of product that appear on the supermarket shelves under different labels.

A large bakery, for example, may produce meat pies. As the pies come out of the oven they are put onto conveyor belts which enclose them in a distinctive Cellophane wrapping with the bakery's brand name on. But then, every so often, the worker operating the conveyor belt will change the Cellophane wrapping. The same pies, made of the same ingredients, baked in the same oven, will then be sold in different wrappings, under different names, at different prices. Then each of the brands will launch expensive advertising campaigns informing us that brand X is tastier than any other brand, or brand Y is healthier, or brand Z is better for your sex life.

We are told capitalism offers variety and choice. Certainly, the range of products on sale in the average superstore can be baffling. One retail chain claims to stock 150,000 different items. But much of the choice on offer is fictitious. The variety is not in the content, but in the packaging, which is often more expensive than the product inside. It is no accident that the richest man in Britain, Hans Rausing, a billionaire four times over, made his fortune in the packaging industry.

Only on the basis of social ownership of industry, energy, transport construction and finance, would it be possible to build an integrated, harmonious, democratically planned economy. Socialism is not about reducing choice; it is about reducing waste and duplication. People living in drought-stricken regions of Africa would find it bizarre that companies in Canada produce bottled water, which they then export thousands of miles across the Atlantic to be sold in shops in rainswept Scotland, a country which needs more water as urgently as Saudi Arabia needs more sand.

In a socialist economy, run by the people for the people, there would be a shift away from global imports of low-quality and unnecessary goods towards locally produced, high-quality, low-cost products. There would be a war on waste as well as a war on poverty.

The Nazi propagandist, Josef Goebbels once made the point that with sufficient repetition it would be possible to 'prove' that a square is actually a circle. By endlessly repeating the claim that private ownership equals efficiency while public ownership equals incompetence, the masters of free-market propaganda have succeeded in turning a dubious assertion into an irrefutable fact.

The entire case for private ownership over social ownership hinges on a couple of flimsy pieces of evidence. The first of these is that the nationalised economies of the Soviet Union and Eastern Europe failed. And the second is that the industries nationalised in the past by Old Labour were inefficient and unprofitable.

These accusations are at least partially justified, but they miss the point. Presenting the failure of bureaucratic nationalisation as proof that democratic social ownership won't work is like reciting William McGonagall to prove that Robert Burns was a dreadful poet. Socialism is not Stalinism with a dose of democracy, nor is it capitalism with a dose of bureaucratic nationalisation.

There is an old saying, 'two wrongs don't make a right'. When pro-capitalist commentators crow about the failure of the Soviet Union, they should remember that two failures don't make a success. Stalinism failed; there is no dispute about that. But capitalism and private ownership have also failed throughout most of the world. Across Asia, Africa, Latin America – where most of the world's population actually lives – capitalism has been a catastrophic failure. It has been unable to provide even the basic necessities of life, such as food, shelter, medicine and water, to countless millions in numerous countries. In Eastern Europe, too, the restoration of private ownership has been, if anything, an even more spectacular failure than Stalinism. It has failed so badly that there is even a large and growing minority who despairingly hark back to the 'good old days' of Brezhnev and Kosygin.

The forms of social ownership appropriate for Scotland in the 21st century will bear no resemblance to the monolithic state-run corporations established by the Old Labour governments of the mid 20th century. These were cumbersome bureaucracies, usually run on autocratic lines by managers drafted in from the private sector. Accountants who knew nothing about the railway system were appointed to run British Rail. Bankers who knew nothing about mining were put in charge of the coal industry. Stockbrokers who knew nothing about the electricity grid were put in charge of power generation. Nothing extraordinary there, that's exactly how these industries are run today under private ownership. One important difference, however is that for all their failings, the nationalised industries were not run purely for profit. In fact, the 1945–51 Labour government which nationalised the railways, the mines, and the power stations, instructed these industries to break even financially. This meant they were able provide better wages and conditions for their workers. It meant they were able keep prices down. It meant they were able to plough investment back into the industry. In other words, they were able do all the things that the previous private owners had failed to do.

Most of the old nationalised industries had been reduced to ruin by their former private owners, who had greedily gobbled up any profits that were made, while starving their businesses of investment.

Most of these companies were on the brink of bankruptcy before they were bought over for exorbitant sums of money by the state.

The newly nationalised industries then proceeded to subsidise the rest of private industry and commerce by providing cheap materials, services, and transportation to big business. At the same time, public investment was poured into these nationalised industries to restore them to health.

Then along came Margaret Thatcher, who sold them back to the private profiteers. And here we come to a strange paradox: industries which were bought by the government for astronomically *inflated* prices when they were bankrupt were now sold by the government at astronomically *deflated* prices after they became profitable.

One of the first public assets sold off by Thatcher was British Telecom. In 1985, it was sold for a rock-bottom £4 billion. In the last five years alone, British Telecom shareholders have piled up four times that amount in profit, £16 billion. You couldn't find a better bargain in Paddy's Market.

Railtrack was sold off in 1996 for £1.9 billion. Within two years the value of the company on the stock exchange was over £8 billion, four and a half times the price it had been sold for in the first place. In total, 60 separate enterprises were sold off by the Tories, and the City fat cats licked their lips with delight. They bought up shares as though they were buying Lottery tickets imprinted with the words 'Jackpot win guaranteed'.

Seven of Scotland's ten biggest companies have made their fortunes, not by developing their own unique products, but by grabbing their slice of the privatised bus, power, and telecommunications industries. Privatisation, and its New Labour offshoots, PFI and PPP, have turned Britain into a profiteers' paradise.

The whole privatisation rip-off was perhaps best summed up, not by any politician, but by the brilliant comic impersonator Rory Bremner. In one of his sketches, a man sits in a pub staring glumly into his pint.

'What's up?' says his drinking companion.

'I got my car stolen last night,' replies the man morosely. 'And, even worse, the guy that stole it came round to my door and offered to sell it to me.'

'But that's theft!' says his mate.

'No,' he replies. 'That's privatisation!'

In the book, *A Future for Public Ownership*, two Leeds University academics, Malcolm Sawyer and Kath O'Donnell, blow apart the myth that private enterprise is more dynamic and successful than public enterprise. They show, for example, that the growth rate was actually *higher* in public enterprises than in privately owned manufacturing industry between 1951 and 1985.

In one American study, which compared American private and public electricity companies, the researchers (Millward and Packer, 1983) concluded that 'none of the cost studies support the proposition that public electricity firms have a lower productivity or higher unit costs than private firms.'[5]

A further study (Yarrow, 1986) concluded that, far from private companies being more efficient, 'the evidence in examples such as electricity supply tends to point in the other direction, towards better performance by public firms.'[6]

Under capitalism, the efficiency of a company is measured by profit and share value. But there is no direct relationship between a company's share value and its social value. Some of the most profitable companies are those which pay low wages to their workforces, rip off their customers, drive their smaller rivals to the wall, pollute the environment, and devour the natural resources of the planet. Similarly, economists judge whether a national economy is 'efficient' or 'inefficient' by totting up crude figures measuring economic growth. But these statistics never tell us what's being produced, why it's being produced, how it's being produced, or whether it benefits or damages society. One country can achieve sky-high growth rates during a war by turning over the whole economy to armaments production. The people of that country may be living in hovels and surviving on bowls of rice but the economy is flourishing because the statistics say so.

Another country can achieve high growth rates because its workers toil from dawn to dusk manufacturing training shoes or motor cars which are then exported abroad because the people who make these things are too poor to buy them. But the business magazines hail this country as 'an economic miracle' because its growth rates seem impressive to those who are impressed by high numbers.

In neither case is there any connection between economic growth and the social health of the nation. A socially owned economy would abandon these accountants' yardsticks and set new criteria by which to gauge the health of society and the performance of individual enterprises that operate within that society.

These criteria would be based not on what benefits share-holders, but on what benefits the public. Industry, services, transport, energy, construction would be geared towards social need rather than private greed. People would become more important than profit. Protection of the natural environment would become more important than columns of figures on a balance sheet.

To put forward such a radical vision of a different type of economy is to invite ridicule from some quarters and provoke terror in other quarters. Smug politicians will shake their heads wisely as though to say, 'These socialists really do live in a dream world.' Some businessmen will throw up their hands in horror at the outlandish suggestion that ordinary people could actually take over the economy and run it themselves. How could mere human beings ever replace these supermen and wonderwomen who understand business, who are able read balance sheets, who know how to order people around, who know exactly what they're doing.

Supermen like Lord Weinstock, for example, who on the day of his retirement in early 2000 admitted in an interview with the *Financial Times* that he had never once set foot in any GEC factory in his 30 years as managing director of the company!

Part Three

POWER TO THE PEOPLE

Say you want a revolution
We better get on right away
Well you get on your feet
And out on the street
Singing Power to the People.

Chapter Eleven

FROM RED FLAG
TO WHITE RAG

IT'S FAST-FORWARD TO the year 2010 and the Tories are back in government. After losing the 2001 general election, the party reinvented itself. First it decided to break out of the ghetto of its suburban heartlands and began to champion instead the rights of the working class and the poor. The New Tory Party was born. It elected as its leader a former miner from Tyneside who spoke with a broad Geordie accent and had been educated at his local state comprehensive school.

Gradually, the party turned its back on its traditional supporters, the rich and powerful. New Tory leaders began to write articles in the *Scottish Socialist Voice*, the *Morning Star*, and other left-wing publications, arguing that capitalism was now 'irrelevant and out of date'. They toured trade-union conferences winning rapturous applause for their assurances that the Tory Party had become the new party of the working class and the trade unions.

When he eventually swept to power, the New Tory leader appointed a range of left-wing trade-union activists to key Cabinet posts. 'We live in a class-ridden society,' he declared as he unveiled his plan to bring back into public ownership the assets that had been privatised by previous governments. The New Tory government then set about levying punitive taxes on big business and establishing special anti-fraud squads designed to root out tax embezzlement by the rich. Tory candidates who protested against these measures or dared to praise capitalism or private profiteering were branded as traitors to the New Tory project and driven out of the party.

Far-fetched? Maybe. Except that it's already happened – in reverse. Tony Blair likes to portray himself as a radical pioneer, bravely blazing a new trail into unexplored territory. As everyone knows, the Labour leader is addicted to the word 'New'. Every speech is peppered with references to the New Millennium, the New Century, New Britain, the New Economy, New Thinking, New Ideas, New Politics, New Policies, New Labour. In one interview, he even managed to make a reference to 'our New Traditions'.

But there is nothing at all new about New Labour. It is old Toryism in a New Suit, Thatcherism with a grinning face. Tony Blair is in essence a political used-car salesman, who has taken the battered old wreck of Thatcherism, painted over the rust, and changed the mileage on the clock.

Tony Blair makes no bones about where he stands. 'The old ideological conflict between Left and Right is over,' he claims. 'The conflict between capital and labour is a thing of the past.' These are remarkable statements from the leader of a political party that was formed by the trade unions to provide political representation for the working class. It is like the Pope declaring that 'the old theological conflict between Christianity and atheism is over', or the scientist Stephen Hawkins announcing that 'the law of gravity is a thing of the past'.[1]

Many socialists hold Blair personally responsible for tearing out the party's socialist heart and soul. They contrast him with the first-ever Labour leader. James Keir Hardie was a cautious and moderate man, a devoted Christian, and a fierce supporter of the temperance movement, to boot. Beside Blair, his courage shines out like brilliant sunshine beside a flickering candle.

Keir Hardie lashed out against injustice at every turn. He backed the Suffragettes, demanded that the rich be taxed to the hilt, denounced inherited privilege, lambasted the monarchy and opposed the imperialist slaughter of the First World War. He backed independence for India 50 years before it was granted and denounced apartheid in South Africa 80 years before the system was finally dismantled.

The Tory press barons of the day hated and feared Keir Hardie with a vengeance. They daily spewed out vitriol against this former Lanarkshire miner, who had been sent out to become the family breadwinner at the age of seven. Hardie merely shrugged his shoulders and dismissed the press hysteria-mongers: 'If my enemies start to praise me, that's when I'll start to worry.'

By contrast, Tony Blair is fêted by the rich and powerful. For the pampered privileged minority who own Britain, Tony is 'one of us', a man who can be trusted wholeheartedly to stand on the side of wealth and power when the chips are down.

The transnational press baron, Rupert Murdoch, whose UK subsidiary, News Corporation, makes a £1 billion a year profit and fails to pay a penny tax to the British Exchequer, is worshipped like a king by the New Labour leader. Blair's closest political associates include grocery tycoon, Lord Sainsbury; multimillionaire stockbroker, Gavyn Davies; Lord Simon, who butchered 65,000 jobs at BP; Virgin boss, Richard Branson; motor-racing billionaire, Bernie Ecclestone; and former media mogul, Lord Gus MacDonald.

But, although Tony Blair may appear as the living embodiment of the Tory takeover of Labour, there are far more powerful forces shaping New Labour than spin doctors and used-car salesmen. The New Labour project is part of a wholesale international migration from Left to Right as a vast procession of former workers' parties across Europe tear down the red flag and hoist the white handkerchief.

Far from standing in the vanguard of 'modernisation', New Labour is lagging behind its Spanish counterpart by almost two decades. Felipe Gonzales, the leader of PSOE, the Spanish Socialist Workers' Party, was a Blairite when Tony Blair himself still professed to be a socialist. Under Gonzales, Spanish unemployment rose to 22 per cent, and his party is back in opposition.

In Portugal, Greece, Germany, Sweden, and a host of other countries across Europe and further afield – for example, Australia and New Zealand – an identical process has occurred. Parties which once proudly described themselves as 'socialist', or at least as social democratic, have turned into fervent free-marketers.

This mass capitulation to capitalism is not simply a product of copy-cat politics. It is rooted in the changes in the global capitalist economy over the past few decades, which leave no scope for muddled moderation.

In the 1930s, the poetic genius Hugh MacDiarmid wrote: 'I'll hae nae haufway hoose; I'll aye be whaur extremes meet.'[2] This could be the leitmotif of global politics in the 21st century, as snarling capitalism, red in tooth and claw, runs amok.

In the past, Labour proudly proclaimed that its mission was to achieve socialism in Britain. In 1947, the party even published its own centenary edition of the *Communist Manifesto*, the famous clarion call to revolution written by Marx and Engels in the mid 19th century. The foreword declared, 'In presenting this centenary volume of the *Communist Manifesto*, the Labour Party acknowledges its indebtedness to Marx and Engels as two men who have been the inspiration of the whole working class movement.'

In reality, although Labour was a socialist party in words, it was, in practice, a social democratic party. Social democracy was in essence a more restrained and civilised version of the capitalist free market. It's aim was to reform capitalism, to make the system more just, more humane, more concerned for the welfare of the poor.

Governments based on these principles did introduce important reforms that vastly improved the quality of life of ordinary people. In Britain, the 1945–51 Labour government imposed hefty taxes on the rich. It introduced the two greatest social reforms carried out by any government in the 300-year history of the British state – the welfare state and the National Health Service.

In Germany and Scandinavia, reforming governments poured resources into health, housing, education, pensions, and welfare. For decades on end, social democracy reigned supreme throughout most of Northern Europe, with even Tory governments adapting themselves to this left-of-centre post-war consensus.

These governments also began to move away from unbridled free-market capitalism. Some essential loss-making industries and services were nationalised. In Britain, coal, steel, electricity, gas, and the railways were taken over by the state. This was termed 'the mixed economy'.

But pouring a bottle of whisky into Loch Katrine doesn't transform it into a mixed reservoir. Nor is it possible to achieve semi-socialism. The essential ingredients of socialism – mass democracy social equality, and a co-ordinated harmonious economy – were absent in these societies. The new nationalised industries were run as bureaucratic monopolies while the bulk of these 'mixed economies' continued to be run from the boardrooms and stock exchanges.

In Britain, the social democrats were not even genuine social democrats. Feudal institutions such as the monarchy and the House of Lords continued to thrive under a succession of Labour governments. Inherited wealth and privilege remained woven into the fabric of British society.

Some reforming Labour politicians did have grander ambitions. The best of these had the idea that it would be possible to evolve gradually towards some form of socialism. In the words of a post-war parody of the socialist anthem, 'The Red Flag', 'We'll change the country bit by bit; so nobody will notice it.' But instead of crawling forward towards socialism, Labour governments in Britain and abroad have since galloped backwards towards classical free-market Toryism.

The start of this process can be traced back as far as the mid-1970s, when the long gentle upward curve of capitalism was abruptly interrupted by an earth-shattering economic crisis. In Britain, a Labour government had been elected in 1974, pledged to carry out 'a fundamental and irreversible shift in the balance of wealth and power in favour of working people and their families'. It also pledged to bring about full employment, an expansion of public services, increased pensions and benefits, and the nationalisation of North Sea oil and other key sectors of the economy.[3]

By 1979, when Labour left office, there were twice as many people unemployed as there had been in 1974. With the unelected bankers of the International Monetary Fund holding a gun to its head, the Labour government had forced through the biggest programme of cuts in health, education, and local-government expenditure ever seen in post-war Britain. It had mobilised the army onto the streets to break strikes of binmen and firefighters.

North Sea oil and other sectors of the economy, which Labour had promised to nationalise, remained in big-business hands. Instead of a redistribution of wealth and power from rich to poor, there took place a redistribution of wealth and power from poor to rich. The government finally crumbled in the wake of the so-called 'Winter of Discontent', when the patience of millions of pitifully low-paid public-sector workers finally snapped.

From then on, nothing was ever the same again. Thatcher took power, and the long post-war consensus was ripped to shreds. She waged the most vicious social war ever seen in post-war Europe against the working class and its organisations. But, like Blair today, Thatcher was merely implementing an agenda dictated by the needs of an economic system battling for survival. To one degree or another, the same agenda was pursued across Europe, North and South America, and Australasia.

In a bizarre historical twist, some of the most rabidly Thatcherite governments on the planet had originally been elected as workers' parties committed to social democracy. In New Zealand, for example, a Labour government went further than even Thatcher dared to venture. Hospitals and schools were converted into commercial businesses; taxes on big business and the rich were cut by 50 per cent; collective bargaining was effectively outlawed with every worker in the public and private sector placed on an individual contract. One of the most comprehensive welfare states in the world was whittled down to a Latin American level.

In Europe too, the same trend unfolded, although never carried through to the same extreme as in New Zealand. In Britain, the political centre of gravity has shifted so far to the right that even an old-style Labour moderate such as Lord Hattersley is now ridiculed within his own party as a left-wing dinosaur. Even in its Scandinavian heartlands, social democracy has been abandoned.

In the ferocious new world of hi-tech, turbocharged, de-regulated global capitalism, the international political and business elite has decided there is no longer any room for sentimental notions such as social justice or wealth redistribution.

Following a meeting of the World Economic Forum attended by 1000 top corporate executives in January 2000, the respected British economist. Will Hutton, who yearns for a return to some form of social democracy, observed, 'It would take an intellectual atom bomb along with gigantic riots to force global business leaders to change course.'[4]

Professor John Gray, yet another fierce critic of unregulated free-market capitalism, is even more pessimistic: 'Social democracy has been removed from the agenda of history.' He argues that 'many of the changes produced, accelerated or reinforced by New Right policies are irreversible ... Those who imagine that there can be a return to the "normal politics" of post-war economic management are deluding themselves and others ... Global mobility of capitalism has made the central policies of European social democracy unworkable.'[5]

When New Labour Chancellor Gordon Brown intones that 'there will be no return to the old tax-and-spend policies of the past', he is simply reciting his lines. The script is no longer written by chancellors or prime ministers; it is written by corporate vampires who are no longer prepared to pay taxes to finance extravagant spending on such fripperies as welfare benefits, health, and education. As the famous economist JK Galbraith points out, 'The rich are no longer prepared to pay for the poor.'[6]

There is nothing that any government can do to alter that – other than stand up to the rich and challenge the very existence of the global capitalist system. Sadly, there is as much likelihood of New Labour taking such a stance as there is of Bill Gates donating his entire personal fortune to Oxfam.

Chapter Twelve

DR JEKYLL, MR HYDE . . . AND THE SNP

DURING THE 1980S, Margaret Thatcher strutted the world stage pronouncing platitudes about the rights of small nations from Afghanistan to Kuwait, from the Baltic States to the Falkland Islands. Meanwhile, she treated with ice-cold contempt the demand from 80 per cent of Scots for some measure of Home Rule.

Since then, New Labour has conceded a modest measure of devolution to Scotland and an even more modest measure of devolution to Wales. Contrary to the mythology manufactured by the spin doctors and lazily lapped up by the media, that did not occur because Tony Blair woke up one morning with a bold vision to modernise the United Kingdom. Blair simply inherited a policy which he could not possibly jettison without delivering Scotland gift-wrapped into the grateful arms of the SNP.

From the day he took over as leader of the Labour Party, Blair was lukewarm about the idea of a Scottish Parliament. Along with his coterie of spin doctors and advisers, the New Labour leader has always privately viewed devolution as a ticking time-bomb that could blow up in the face of the UK government at some point in the future. If it were not for the inevitable political fallout, Blair would gladly have dumped devolution into the political dustbin labelled 'outdated dogma' alongside public ownership, trade-union rights, and opposition to privatisation.

Instead he watered down Labour's devolution proposals to render them less dangerous. For example, under the plan drawn up by the Labour-dominated Scottish Constitutional Convention in 1995, the Scottish Parliament would have had the power 'to take land, property and enterprises into public control and ownership'. This was deleted from New Labour's final blueprint. The Convention's plan for the Scottish Parliament to be responsible for all revenues raised in Scotland was also ditched and replaced by a block grant system from Westminster.

Blair's fears have actually been proven well-founded. Instead of 'killing off stone-dead the rump demand for separatism', as former Scottish Labour leader George Robertson proclaimed in a fit of bravado, devolution has accelerated the momentum towards the break-up of the UK. The SNP is in a stronger position than ever before in its 66-year history.

As time goes on, the limitations of the devolved Scottish Parliament are become more and more clear to more and more people. A year after the parliament was established, an opinion poll commissioned by Scottish Television found that 78 per cent of Scots believed it had made 'no difference at all' to their lives. Only two per cent of those polled thought that the parliament had done a 'a great deal of good'.

Pro-independence socialists and nationalists have argued all along that the parliament set up by New Labour was inadequate to deal with Scotland's problems.

It has no power to increase pensions or welfare benefits. It has no power to close down the nuclear bases on the Clyde. It has no power to impose a wealth tax on the rich. It has no power to repeal the most repressive anti-trade-union laws in Europe. It has no power to increase the derisory minimum wage. It has no power to bring privatised industries and services back into the public sector. It has no power to take over ownership of North Sea oil, or land, or finance. It has no power to raise the billions of pounds needed to create a modern education system for the 21st century, or build a health service able to cope with a population that is living longer than ever before, or initiate a housing programme that will rid Scotland forever of the scourge of homeless and slum housing.

Scotland needs a proper grown-up parliament, able to take its own decisions on all the issues that matter. Instead, it has been landed with a PG-certificate parliament in which all the big decisions are taken by the grown-ups down in Westminster.

Such an arrangement is a recipe for wholesale disappointment with Holyrood. But that disillusionment won't lead backwards towards the ultra-centralised British state that generated such bitterness under Thatcher and Major; it will lead forward to the goal of a fully independent Scotland.

For those fighting back against capitalism, the disintegration of the United Kingdom should be a cause for celebration rather than for mourning. In a keynote speech designed to bolster the Union Tony Blair gushed about the 'qualities of British identity'. Britishness, he said, is about 'creativity built on tolerance, openness and adaptability, work and self-improvement, strong communities and families and fair play, rights and responsibilities'.[1]

Most nations and states in the world today would also lay claim to these virtues. The suggestion that they are uniquely British is a breathtakingly arrogant assumption that appears to imply that Spaniards and Swedes and Belgians are intolerant, closed-minded, inflexible, lazy, unfair, and irresponsible.

The people who live on this island have no inbred monopoly on the virtues that Blair lists. Indeed, Blair's one-sided presentation of Britain as a paragon of decency and civilised behaviour would be treated as black humour in those parts of the world which were brutally subjugated and their natural resources plundered by British imperialism. Nor is it accurate to claim that there is a single British identity. More than ever before, Britain is a fragmented multinational state, which includes within its borders a diverse multitude of national, regional, cultural, linguistic, and ethnic identities.

In itself, that is not necessarily a bad thing. In the mists of the future, there will be new multinational arrangements, including federations and confederations where resources are shared and integrated on the basis of international common ownership. The legendary Clydeside socialist, John MacLean, while calling for a Scottish Socialist Republic simultaneously offered a vision of a world without borders in which 'intermarriage will wipe out all national differences and the world will become one'.[2]

But the British state is not a step towards a socialist world. It is essentially a reactionary and conservative institution, which acts as a gigantic brake on social and political progress. From the outset, Britain was an imperial state which pillaged its way across the globe. The sun may have long since set on the British Empire, and the stone-faced Victorian autocrats may have made way for smiling happy-clappy New Labourites, but the UK today remains one of the chief bulwarks of world capitalism. For the past 20 years, Britain has stood shoulder-to-shoulder with the United States in its crusade to globalise, privatise, deregulate, and generally turn the planet into the private property of the transnational corporations.

With its nuclear weapons and other military bases, its oil wealth, its landmass, and its financial institutions, Scotland is a key component part of the United Kingdom. The secession of Scotland from the Union would be a shattering defeat for British capitalism, as potent in its historic symbolism as the break-up of the Soviet Union.

But could Scotland really go it alone? Should Scotland go it alone? Could Scotland survive as an independent state? Would it become an economic wasteland, as New Labour and the Liberal Democrats claim? Or would it become a Tartan Tiger, an economic powerhouse, where economic growth would be combined with social reform to produce a society based on 'enterprise and compassion', as the SNP claim?

For the unionist parties, Scottish independence means Apocalypse Now. Before the Scottish parliamentary election in 1999, the Scottish Labour leader, Donald Dewar, predicted a £15 billion deficit over four years if Scotland chose independence. This would mean, according to Dewar, either cutting back public spending by a quarter or increasing the basic rate of income tax by 20 pence in the pound to plug the gap. Either way, Scotland would sink into a swamp of depression and improverishment with hundreds of thousands of jobs lost and a human tidal wave of economic refugees flooding over the border to escape mass unemployment and punitive taxation.

The SNP, naturally, disputes this analysis. They retaliate by claiming that, over the past 20 years, Scotland has subsidised the rest of the UK to the tune of £27 billion. They point out that Scotland is the seventh richest country in the world, as measured by Gross Domestic Product per head of population.

Most people scratch their heads in bewilderment when faced with these claims and counter-claims. Clearly, both sides can't be right. Either New Labour is indulging in crude scaremongering, or the SNP is attempting to seduce the people of Scotland with false promises. So who's right and who's wrong?

The truth is, neither Labour nor the SNP are in a position to predict with any degree of certainly the future prospects for an independent Scotland. There's a saying that if you laid every economist end to end, they would never reach a conclusion. Even with detailed facts and figures at their fingertips, the average economist is about as reliable as the average racing tipster. Attempting to predict the future economic health of a nation-state which does not yet exist is like trying to predict which horse will win the Derby in five years' time.

The facts, figures, and percentages reeled off by New Labour and the SNP are designed to create the impression of scientific objectivity. But there are lies, damned lies, and statistics. For example, Donald Dewar's forecast that an independent Scotland would run up an astronomical £15 billion deficit over four years was made at a time when oil prices were at the lowest level, in real terms, since the early 1970s. But during the following six months, there was a dramatic turnaround. By the start of 2000, oil prices and revenues had risen to their highest levels since the Iraqi invasion of Kuwait sent oil prices into the stratosphere in 1990. Later in 2000, they began to fall back again.[3]

The Scottish economy is especially susceptible to fluctuations in the price of oil. Invariably, the unionist parties base their projections for an independent Scotland on the *lowest* possible oil prices, while the SNP, naturally, bases its projections upon the *highest* possible oil prices.

The famous £27 billion surplus claimed by the SNP mainly relates to the years between 1979 and 1985, when oil revenues were sky-high due to the high price of crude oil and the more rigorous tax regime then in operation. Since then, the position has become much more complicated. A line graph produced by the Royal Bank of Scotland charting the fluctuations in oil prices between 1983 and 2000 looks like a photo negative of the Cuillins, with high peaks, deep gorges and precipitous drops. As the bank's oil economists point out, 'it is not sensible to forecast oil prices'.[4]

Similarly, when the SNP claims that Scotland is the seventh richest country in the world, they are playing with statistics that tend to fluctuate dramatically from one month to the next. In any case, crude figures for GDP do not accurately measure overall living standards. They include profits amassed by foreign-owned companies and then shipped overseas. Scotland's GDP includes the profits made by North Sea oil companies, which are American-, Dutch- and English-owned. These profits may be made in Scotland but they are immediately salted away into overseas bank accounts.

Many people rightly support independence because they believe that an independent Scotland would be more egalitarian, more left-wing, more socialist in outlook than 'Cruel Britannia'. Certainly, the balance of forces in Scotland is more heavily weighted in favour of the working class than in Britain as a whole. The influence of socialism is deeper. The forces of right-wing conservatism are weaker. Social attitudes tend to be more progressive. The political centre of gravity is significantly further to the left.

Operating in such a climate, the SNP takes great care to present itself as a left-of-centre alternative to New Labour. These days, that is no difficult feat. In fact, as New Labour has evolved further and further to the right, it has been stalked in the background by the New SNP. Taking care never to actually catch up or overtake New Labour, the SNP has nonetheless shifted rightwards on a whole range of policies over the past decade.

In the 1992 general election, the SNP called for the single person's pension to be raised to £90 a week. Any reasonable person would assume that, by 1997, pensioners would need more money to survive, given the rising cost of living. But not the SNP leadership. By 1997, the party was promising pensioners £65 a week – £25 less than five years before.

In the early 1990s, the SNP stood for the bringing back into public ownership of industries such as electricity and gas, and vehemently opposed the sell-off of the rail industry. By the end of the 1990s, companies like Railtrack and ScottishPower, which piled up vast profit mountains from the privatisation rip-off, were sponsoring the SNP conference. All references to public ownership have now been purged from party policy statements, programmes, and manifestos

Most people would also expect the SNP to be a republican

party. The British monarchy is one of the most conservative and reactionary institutions in the world. It reeks of feudal patronage and privilege. A verse of the royalist national anthem, 'God Save the Queen' even boasts about crushing 'rebellious Scots'. Yet the extraordinarily subservient SNP leadership never tire of reassuring the British establishment that, under their proposals, an independent Scotland will remain a monarchy with the Queen as head of state.

While insisting that they are 'social democrats', the SNP leadership has also repeatedly flirted with right-wing economic theories imported from America. The party has strongly hinted that it would like to reduce corporation tax on big business from 30 per cent to 12.5 per cent, even though the current level of corporation tax in the UK is already one of the lowest in Europe.

The SNP invokes the work of right-wing American economist Arthur Laffer to justify its support for handing over billions of pounds of public money to wealthy business corporations. Laffer, a guru of Reaganomics in the 1980s, argues that tax cuts, under certain conditions, can stimulate investment and production and, as a result, yield more overall tax. The SNP point to the astounding growth of the Irish economy as a model that could be emulated by an independent Scotland.

But the rise of the 'Celtic Tiger' took place against the background of a general upswing in the world economy, which is now reaching its limits. The Irish economy has also been fuelled by massive cash injections from the European Union, which are about to dry up. Many American and Asian transnational companies were attracted into the Irish Republic by low taxes, cheap labour, lavish government grants, and access to the European Union. Measured by bare statistics, the growth of the Irish economy has been extraordinary. But the Irish Republic continues to languish near the bottom of the European poverty league table. Now a cluster of Eastern European countries are queueing up to join the European Union, and they are able to offer even cheaper labour, even lower taxes, and even more generous subsidies.

The idea that business can be bribed to invest is one-sided and naïve. Business will only invest in any industry when it knows there are profitable markets to exploit. In the new conditions opening up across Europe, a tax-cutting policy in a capitalist independent Scotland would mean transferring billions from public services into the private bank accounts of wealthy shareholders.

Some key figures within the SNP go even further than the leadership in promoting the type of economic policies which have led to mass destitution across Latin America and other parts of the world. The party's former environment spokesperson, George Kerevan, a former Labour councillor, advocates turning Scotland into a tartan paradise for investors. He proposes abolishing the top rate of income tax and introducing a 20 per cent flat rate across Scotland, which would mean a cleaner on £4.00 an hour paying the same rate of taxation as a company director on £400 an hour.[5] It would also mean plundering billions from health, education, and other public services to finance this generous plan to make the rich richer.

Kerevan has also called on Scotland to 'go global', to 'get our retaliation in first and build our own multinationals'. He complains that 'Scotland has only half as many global companies per head as the UK, and a quarter as many as other small European nations such as Austria and Switzerland'.[6]

But the number of multinational, or transnational, companies operating on the world markets is not growing; it is diminishing, as they gobble each other up like corporate cannibals. In any case, how exactly would such an economic strategy benefit ordinary people within Scotland? When companies 'go global', they expand their operations to those parts of the world where they can find the cheapest labour and the lowest taxes.

As a general rule, the transnational corporations are becoming less and less dependent on their home countries. The Canadian-based transnational empire Seagram, which distils Chivas Regal, Glen Grant, Glen Isla, 100 Pipers, the Glenlivet and other Scotch whisky brands, conducts 97 per cent of its operation abroad with only a small core workforce based at its Montreal headquarters. The American footwear colossus Nike does not manufacture a single pair of shoes in its home country.

The entire history of the SNP is one of twists, turns, and zigzags. Like a marching regiment, the SNP rank and file are expected to fall into step with the orders of the leadership at every turn: 'Left! Right! Left! Right!'

Today the party combines a right-wing economic policy with a left-of-centre social policy. It promises lavish tax handouts to big business. It simultaneously promises generous increases in spending on public services. Presumably, under an SNP government, Santa Claus will be appointed Chancellor of the Exchequer.

The harsh truth is that there is no room for charity or sentiment in the capitalist jungle of the 21st century. Attempting to promote left-wing social policies while pursuing right-wing economic policies is like trying to walk forward with one leg and backwards with the other. The result, for the SNP and for anyone else who attempts such a feat, will be a painful rupture.

Chapter Thirteen

CHAMPAGNE AND CYANIDE

IN THE 1950s, after the Authors' Union of East Germany, a front for the ruling Communist Party, published a leaflet condemning a general strike of workers, the celebrated poet and playwright, Bertolt Brecht, wrote:

> 'After the Uprising on June 17th
> The Secretary of the Authors' Union
> Had leaflets distributed in the
> Stalinallee which said that the people
> Had forfeited the government's confidence
> And could only win it back
> By redoubled labour. Wouldn't it
> Be simpler in that case if the government
> Dissolved the people and
> Elected another?'[1]

For socialists, democracy is not an optional extra, like a preference for sugar in tea. Socialism without free elections, without free trade unions, without free speech, is not socialism.

Back in the 19th century, Karl Marx, when he read the policies of a political party that claimed to stand on his ideas, commented: 'If that's Marxism, I'm no Marxist.' In the 20th century, millions of people in the West decided that they were not socialists, even though they instinctively sympathised with the ideals of socialism, such as equality, democracy, co-operation, and solidarity. And the reason they rejected socialism was because they were told that the Soviet Union was a socialist state.

It suited the rulers of the Soviet Union, and of the other states that later modelled themselves on the Soviet Union, to portray themselves as socialist. And it also suited the rulers of the capitalist West to portray these hideously repressive regimes as socialist. 'If you don't like capitalism, that's the alternative – salt mines and labour camps, repression, and uniformity. That's socialism!'

In truth, the Soviet Union and the other drab monolithic states, run by grey bureaucratic cliques, had as much in common with socialism as cyanide has with champagne. Under the rule of the tin-pot dictators who ran these countries, genuine socialist dissidents suffered imprisonment, torture, exile and execution for daring to demand democratic rights.

Meanwhile the bureaucrats who ran these countries and their vast entourage of hangers-on accumulated personal riches beyond the wildest dreams of those they ruled over. When the Ceaucescu government in Romania was toppled on Christmas Day 1989, ordinary Romanians were left stunned at the extent of the personal wealth that this 'communist' dictator and his family had hoarded for themselves. While the mass of population were rationed to a single light bulb, the Ceaucescu family were discovered to have owned thousands of crystal chandeliers. The tyrant had his own personal marble-lined nuclear bunker. He had specially reserved deer forests for hunting, while the mass of the population lived at the edge of starvation.

Absolute equality could never be achieved within the borders of a single country, even one based on the principles of genuine socialism. For a transitional period, at least, differentials in salaries would be necessary to prevent the possibility of a brain-drain of key specialists.

Full economic equality could only be attainable on the basis of an advance in productivity and living standards. This in turn would require the victory of socialism on a continental, or even worldwide, scale and the establishment of an international commonwealth of socialist nations.

But the general trend within any genuine socialist state would be away from inequality towards equality. In the Soviet Union and its Eastern European satellites, the trend was in the opposite direction. The highest stratum in Soviet society had begun to live lifestyles akin to the ruling classes of America and Europe. In the Soviet Union itself, there were 100,000 millionaires under communism. In the late 1980s, it was estimated that three per cent of the population of the country owned 80 per cent of savings in banks.

It was not always that way. In the early days, the original aim of the Russian Revolution had been to blaze the trail towards a new socialist world based on co-operation, equality and democracy. Across Europe, millions of young men were being sent to the mass slaughterhouses of Flanders and Armentiers. Back home, their families were living in abominable slums and suffering terrible poverty. In Russia, the people had for generations lived under the iron heel of Tsarism. When this rotting edifice was brought crashing to the ground in 1917, there was mass jubilation among working people from one end of Europe to the other.

In one country after another, workers' uprisings sought to emulate the Bolshevik revolution in Russia. In Glasgow, the legend of Red Clydeside was born 14 months later, as tens of thousands of workers took on the might of the British government. Panic-stricken, the British Prime Minister Lloyd George mobilised 12,000 troops armed to the teeth with machine guns, tanks and aeroplanes from England into the city and locked up local regiments in Maryhill Barracks for fear they would join the workers' revolt.

In a secret memorandum to the French Prime Minister,

Georges Clemenceau, Lloyd George expressed utter despair: 'The whole of Europe is filled with the spirit of Revolution. There is a deep sense not only of discontent, but of anger and revolt ... The whole existing order in its political, social, and economic aspects is being questioned by the masses of the population from one end of Europe to another'.[2]

But, outside Russia, the forces opposing capitalism lacked the strength, cohesion, and determination to win. The Russian Revolution was left isolated. And trying to build socialism in a backward country like Russia 1917 was like trying to build a fire in a waterlogged swamp in the pouring driving rain without a stick of wood, a teaspoonful of fuel, or a single match. The material foundations for a thriving socialist democracy simply did not exist in a state which still had one foot in the Dark Ages.

As a result, the dream of socialism was usurped by the monstrosity of Stalinism. An entire generation of genuine socialists were systematically annihilated, along with millions of ordinary Russian men and women who perished in the gulags and concentration camps. The same pattern was repeated in one form or another throughout Eastern Europe, and in other totalitarian states, such as China, which later imitated Stalin's Soviet Union.

Without either the whip of the capitalist market or the check of genuine democracy, corruption, waste, and bureaucratic incompetence ran rampant in these states. Yet as a result of the abolition of capitalism, the Soviet Union achieved spectacular social and economic advances. In 1917, the country had been at the same economic level as India. By the 1960s, it had risen to become the world's second industrial and military superpower after the United States.

In the 50 years up to 1963, Soviet industrial output multiplied more than 52 times over. In contrast, over the same period, industrial output in the US grew just six times over, while in

Britain it barely doubled. By the early 1960s, the Soviet Union had risen from a state of medieval barbarism to become the first country in the world to launch an artificial satellite and to send an astronaut into space.

For decades, the Soviet Union competed with and even outstripped the West, industry for industry. Capitalist economists today refer to the 'miraculous' American economic boom of the past eight years with the US economy growing at around three per cent a year. But throughout the whole of the 1950s the Soviet economy grew at an average of *ten* per cent a year. In the 1960s, it grew at seven per cent a year; in the 1970s at five per cent.[3]

Living standards of ordinary people improved phenomenally. From a country where cannibalism was rife in some regions right up until 1917, one in three of the population had a university degree by the 1980s. Gas, electricity, and local telephone calls were provided free. Health, education, and public-sector housing were all of superior quality to the West. In East Germany and European Russia, living standards leapfrogged ahead of Britain.

What made these gains even more incredible was that they were achieved under the suffocating rule of a bureaucratic clique that strangled initiative and stifled individual flair. The ruling bureaucracy also displayed an unhealthy obsession with stark statistics. Social, human, and environmental considerations were subordinated to the achievement of production targets set by Moscow. Vast quantities of unwanted goods were churned out of the factories, while there were permanent shortages of many essential foodstuffs.

The environment was literally laid waste. In some parts of Eastern Europe, the rain that fell from the skies was jet black. In Ceaucescu's Romania, beautiful medieval cathedrals were razed to the ground and replaced with giant concrete blocks, each identical to one another. Babies are still being born today in Belarus and Ukraine with limbs and organs missing as a result of the radioactivity released into the atmosphere when the Chernobyl nuclear reactor exploded in 1986.

Eventually, in the 1980s, even economic growth ground to a halt. As America, under Reagan, intensified the arms to frightening proportions, the Soviet economy was drained of resources as it strove to compete. For a long stretch of the 1980s, the US government was spending a colossal $1 billion a day on armaments. The Soviet government tried to match this expenditure, and bankrupted itself in the process.

At the same time, faced with the technological revolution which first began to unfold in the mid-1970s, the Soviet government stood paralysed with fear, like a rabbit caught in the glare of a car's headlights. In any totalitarian state, information systems are rigidly controlled by the government. In the Soviet Union and Eastern Europe, every typewriter and photocopier had to be registered. No newspapers could be published and no TV or radio programme could be broadcast without official permission.

But no society that relies for survival on mind control could ever be capable of developing information technology, no matter how many brilliant scientists and technicians it has trained. For Orwellian states based on repression and fear, the free flow of information is like a lethal poison surging through the bloodstream.

The stagnation of the Soviet and Eastern European economies from the 1980s onwards paved the way in turn for a huge upsurge of political dissent, which embraced national minorities, environmentalists, and pro-democracy campaigners. Eventually the whole project unravelled, culminating in the tearing down of the Berlin Wall and the disintegration of the Soviet Union itself.

For tens of millions across Eastern Europe, the promised free-market Garden of Eden has turned into a vision of hell. The Scottish journalist, John Lloyd, one of the intellectual cheerleaders of capitalism, set out the stark facts in an article in the *New York Times* in 1999:

> 'Russians, free to get richer, are poorer. The wealth of the nation has shrunk. The top 10 per cent is reckoned to possess 50 per cent of the nation's wealth; the bottom 40 per cent less than 20. Somewhere between 30 and 40 million people live below the poverty line – defined as around $30 a month. The gross domestic product has shrunk every year except one – 1997 – when it grew, at best by one per cent. Unemployment, officially non-existent in Soviet times, is now 12 per cent and may officially be 25 per cent. Men die, on average, in their late 50s. Diseases like tuberculosis and diphtheria have reappeared; servicemen suffer malnutrition; the population shrinks rapidly.'

Welcome to capitalism.

Moscow today is a cross between modern Calcutta, with its teeming poverty, and 1920s Chicago, with its rampant gangsterism. Economists estimate that two thirds of all businesses, 400 banks and several dozen stock exchanges are run by the country's 150 Mafia gangs. Up to 40 per cent of the country's Gross Domestic Product is in the hands of organised crime syndicates.

A new mega-billionaire elite has emerged, ripping off the country's assets right, left, and centre. Ten so-called entrepreneurs are believed to have salted way $1.2 trillion in Swiss banks while the Russian economy fell apart. The most notorious member of this new 'kleptocracy' is Boris Berezovsky, known as 'the Godfather of the Kremlin'. Berezovsky owns banks, TV stations, newspapers, oil companies, car dealerships, and airlines. He has a 150-strong private army, many of them KGB-trained assassins and, according to the influential *Forbes* magazine, 'he has left a trail of corpses in his wake'.[4]

As it happens, Mr Berezovsky's closest business collaborator is a well-known international celebrity. Step forward, Rupert Murdoch, the Australian-turned-American Thatcherite-turned-Blairite media mogul.

Prior to 1990, the Soviet Union was neither socialist nor capitalist. A feudal-style hierarchy of rank and privilege was grafted onto a grotesquely centralised command economy. Although the top tiers of this hierarchy owned vast wealth, they were not capitalists in the proper sense of the word. A capitalist is not just someone who is wealthy. In the West today, there are wealthy pop stars, film stars, and footballers, but Elton John, Sean Connery, and David Beckham are not capitalists. Their wealth does not derive from ownership of stocks and shares, or from employing and exploiting the labour of other people, as is the case with a capitalist.

In the former Soviet Union, there were no stock exchanges before the 1990s. But, like caterpillars turning into butterflies, an army of Stalinist bureaucrats turned themselves into private capitalists as the Russian economy was privatised.

An article in *The Economist* in 1994 pointed out that the Young Communist League (the Komsomol) 'is the Harvard or Yale of the new business culture, churning out privileged entrepreneurs ... Komsomol leaders have set up huge commercial banks that are beginning to dominate the financial scene.'

In the past, one of the abusive epithets hurled by the media in this country against left-wing socialists was 'Trotskyite'. Most of the journalists who used this term had no understanding of who Leon Trotsky actually was, or what he stood for. In fact, the popular revolutionary leader of 1917 was, in the words of Tony Benn, 'the Soviet Union's first dissident'. In George Orwell's classic work, *Nineteen Eighty-Four* the hero, Emmanuel Goldstein, was based on Leon Trotsky. 'The Book' referred to throughout Orwell's lucid and gripping polemic against totalitarianism was *Revolution Betrayed*, Trotsky's searing indictment of Stalinism.[5]

In the whole of human history, there is no comparable example of such immense resources of power and propaganda being directed against a single individual. Seven of Trotsky's secretaries and four of his children were murdered by the Soviet Union's apparatus of terror. Throughout his long battle against Stalinist tyranny, the capitalist West sided with Stalin. Churchill denounced Trotsky as 'the Ogre of Europe' and praised 'the reasonable Mr Stalin'. The British Labour Party refused to support Trotsky's request for political asylum, as did every government in the world except that of the Republic of Mexico.

In 1940, Trotsky was finally hunted down and assassinated by a Soviet agent. But ideas can't be murdered. Sure, times have moved on. Certainly, the old political slogans of the 1920s and 1930s cannot simply be regurgitated in the new world of the 21st century. Nonetheless, the basic ideals defended by Trotsky – socialist democracy and working-class internationalism – are even more relevant today than they were then. And his critique of Stalinism, as explained in depth in *Revolution Betrayed*, remains to this day the most powerful and plausible explanation of what went wrong in the Soviet Union.

Chapter Fourteen

ALL THE KING'S MEN

BACK IN THE early part of last century, Scotland's street-corner socialist agitators would start an open-air meeting by asking everyone present to check the feet of the person beside them. Anyone wearing shiny polished boots with distinctive markings could be safely assumed to be a police spy. They would be politely asked to remove themselves from the vicinity so that the meeting could proceed.

These days, the covert operations conducted by the forces of the state against so-called 'subversion' are a million times more sophisticated. In his book, *The Political Police in Britain*, published in 1975, Tony Bunyan explained how the names of three million people – more than one in 20 of the population – were filed on a card-index system locked away in the headquarters of shadowy organisations such as Special Branch and MI5. He revealed how the intelligence services would tap telephones, open mail, photograph demonstrators, monitor the left-wing press, photocopy petitions, infiltrate trade unions and political parties, bug their headquarters, and send agent provocateurs to demonstrations.[1]

That was a quarter of a century ago. In the hi-tech 21st century, techniques such as steaming open envelopes and burgling houses to plant listening devices in telephones appear as quaintly dated as the early James Bond films. Nowadays, the state has the capacity to monitor tens of thousands of phone calls simultaneously. For the past ten years, every single phone call, fax, and email sent between Britain and Ireland has been intercepted and sent to the Government Communications Headquarters (GCHQ) for analysis.

A vast array of information is collated from a variety of resources, including phone calls logged by British Telecom, bank account details, credit-card transactions, housing information, vehicle particulars, social-security records, newspapers, the Internet, undercover agents, and paid informants. This, in turn, is used to build up an intricate picture of the lifestyle, habits, and appearance of millions of individuals, right down to their accents and even their shoe sizes.

The people who conduct these operations are unelected by anyone, and unaccountable to the general public. They are operate under conditions of total secrecy in a clandestine sub-world which is beyond the control even of elected politicians.

The Internet represents an extraordinary breakthrough in communications, allowing a free flow of information and ideas at a speed that would have seemed incomprehensible a few decades ago. But the dark side of the Internet is its potential to provide the framework for the most comprehensive surveillance system ever devised. For example, the British government's RIP Bill will force Internet Service Providers to track every piece of data passing through their computers and route this information to the so-called Government Technical Assistance Centre, an innocent-sounding organisation which is actually a front for MI5.

The government even plans to force people to surrender encryption codes. Encryption is the deliberate scrambling of a file to make it unreadable except by those who know the code. It is the cyber equivalent of a front-door key, or a locker key.[2]

Imagine the police were given powers – without obtaining a warrant or any other form of permission – to force you to hand over your keys to allow them to rifle through your possessions whenever they feel like it. Imagine that the penalty for refusing to hand the keys over was two years in jail. And if that's not sufficiently hair-raising, try to picture a law which left you liable to five years' imprisonment simply for letting someone else know that the police have obtained a copy of their front-door key.

If this sounds far-fetched, it shouldn't. That's the law on encryption codes that the British New Labour government is attempting to steamroller through. Even big business is up in arms at this astounding invasion of personal privacy, although as always, big business has an ulterior motive, a six-letter word beginning with P.

But surely all of this information-gathering is about fighting crime and thwarting terrorism? That's the message that government ministers repeat until they are blue in the face. All of this state snooping, they assure us, is in a good cause: to protect the public from heroin dealers, paedophiles, and bloodthirsty bombers. Believe that, and you could possibly be persuaded that Elvis Presley is alive and well and working as a barman in Brechin.

Of course, it's true that undercover surveillance is used to combat drug trafficking and such-like – though not with a great deal of success, it has to be said. But it would be naive to imagine that's all there is to it. It is an interesting fact that the controversial RIP Bill, with its self-proclaimed goal of bringing state surveillance into the Internet age, is itself an extension of an earlier piece of legislation, the Interception of Communications Act 1985. This act was brought in by the Thatcher government, not as an anti-crime measure, but as an anti-subversion measure.

It was first introduced during the 1984–85 miners' strike and its main purpose was to legitimise the mass telephone tapping of striking miners. It has since been used against a whole range of perfectly legal and respectable organisations, including trade unions, pressure groups, and political parties. The former general secretary of the Scottish Trades Union Congress, Campbell Christie, even took the UK government to the European Court of Human Rights in 1994 to challenge the use of this legislation against the STUC, when it was discovered that telephone calls between Christie's office and overseas trade unionists were being monitored.

In his disturbing book, *The Enemy Within*, Seumas Milne, a highly respected journalist with the *Guardian*, detailed the terrifying lengths to which the British state machine was prepared to go to defeat the miners' strike. During that epic twelve-month conflict, 11,000 miners – one in ten of the entire workforce – were arrested. A total of £6 billion – in today's money, almost the equivalent of the entire annual spending budget of the Scottish Parliament – was poured in by the government to break the strike.

The largest police mobilisations ever seen in the United Kingdom outside of Northern Ireland took place on an almost daily basis for an entire year. Covert army operations were organised. Strikebreakers were secretly funded by the state. The union's assets were seized by the courts. The social-security laws were rewritten in an attempt to starve the strikers back to work. The secret intelligence services established a network of paid informers in every pit village in Britain. Hotels, strike headquarters and even fish-and-chip shops were bugged to enable the security forces to eavesdrop on private conversations. Mass telephone tapping, mail interception, and electronic surveillance operations were set up by GCHQ, MI5, and Special Branch. Agent provocateurs were even sent into the heart of the National Union of Mineworkers in an attempt to disrupt the organisation and frame its leaders on embezzlement charges.[3]

The striking miners were not drug barons or international terrorists. They were not even fighting to topple the government or to overthrow capitalism. Their battle was purely defensive:

to save jobs, stop pit closures, and protect their communities. In other words, they were simply seeking to preserve the status quo.

The question naturally arises: if those are the lengths to which the British Establishment was prepared to go to defeat the miners, what desperate measures might they be prepared to take if faced with a serious challenge to their rule? For example, what would be the reaction of the British state if a socialist government were to be elected in Scotland?

After all, this may be a small country on the outer fringes of the European continent, but it is of enormous strategic importance to the faceless men and women who control the economic, political, and military operations of Western capitalism. Over 80 per cent of the European Union's oil reserves are located in Scottish waters. The city of Edinburgh is the fourth most important financial centre in Europe after London, Frankfurt, and Milan. Meanwhile, Scotland is effectively the 'aircraft carrier' for NATO. It also harbours the biggest nuclear arsenal in Europe and furnishes the Western military alliance with a hugely disproportionate number of army regiments. Above all, Scotland has historically been a crucial component part of the United Kingdom, which for centuries has been one of the chief bulwarks of capitalism worldwide.

The ruling establishment in London and Edinburgh are desperate to hold Britain together and, if that proves impossible in the long term, they will strive with might and main to make sure that any future independent Scotland plays by the rules laid down by global capitalism.

The legendary Celtic and Scotland football coach, the late Jock Stein, used to drum a simple message into the heads of his players: 'Never underestimate the opposition.' Socialists striving to build a new society would do well to apply that advice to the political battlefield.

That doesn't mean cowering before the rich and powerful like frightened schoolchildren hiding away from the school bully. The working class is by far the most numerous and most powerful force in Scotland today. Those with a real stake in capitalism – the stockbrokers and shareholders, the bankers and businessmen, the company directors and chief executives – are a tiny minority of the overall population.

But it would be naïve to imagine that those at the top of the capitalist hierarchy will simply shrug their shoulders and give up their power, prestige, and privileges just because everyone else wants to build a fairer society. A few exceptional individuals may be prepared to sacrifice their personal riches in the interests of social justice, but the majority of the ruling elite are likely to resist change by whatever means necessary.

The British upper classes have always sought to portray themselves as a uniquely civilised decent bunch of people, whose characters were forged on the playing fields of Eton, Rugby, and Gordonstoun where they learned to play fair and accept defeat gracefully.

Most myths are based on a vague glimmer of truth. For 150 years, Britain was a stable capitalist democracy. Britain remained largely inoculated from the high drama that characterised foreign politics; violent revolutions, military coups, civil wars, and fascist dictatorships were regarded as alien to the British way of life.

But Britain's relatively tranquil political climate is not the result of some peculiar characteristic cultivated in the public schools, nor is it due to some genetic twist of fate. Britain's democracy was purchased with the proceeds of the Empire. The respectable and god-fearing British ruling classes waded through oceans of blood abroad – or rather, they paid other people to wade through oceans of blood abroad – in order to accumulate the wealth necessary to buy social peace at home. Although the Empire is long gone, the apparatus of coercion in the hands of the UK Establishment remains formidable. As well as the secret police, it includes the 100,000-strong British Army, the Royal Navy, the RAF, the police, the judiciary, the Civil Service – all institutions which are run from the top down in a rigidly hierarchical fashion by people whose political views tend to place them somewhere to the right of the editors of the *Sun* and the *Daily Telegraph*.

All of this may sound a little bit frightening. After all, if the power of the capitalist state is so immense surely there is no point in even challenging it? Isn't it best just to accept that the balance of forces it so heavily stacked against us that we should give up such a dangerous notion as changing society? Isn't socialism a dangerous road to travel?

All genuine socialists abhor violence. Our goal is to build a society cleansed of all bloodshed and oppression, and we aim to create such a society by peaceful methods. We are confident that the case for socialism will eventually capture the hearts and minds of the majority of Scots, and that our programme of radical socialist change will sooner or later sweep all before it at the ballot box. But let's look forward and try to anticipate the pitfalls and hazards that are strewn ahead. Let's be concrete and imagine it's the year 2010 or 2015 and the forces of democratic socialism have swept to power in a general election, perhaps within an independent Scotland.

What would be the consequences? What happens next? Would there be air strikes launched against Glasgow and Edinburgh by hostile foreign governments? Would a latter-day Edward I lead an invasion force north across the border to re-establish the rule of capitalism in Scotland? Or, alternatively, would the election of a socialist government in Scotland provoke a right-wing military revolt from within?

In politics, as in life generally, it's always necessary to calculate the odds. That's what we do whenever we cross the road, for example, and most of us cross roads every day. It would be foolish to refuse ever to cross a road for fear of the theoretical possibility of being run over. On the other hand, it's always necessary to proceed carefully, paying due regard to the flow of traffic.

As with everyday life, that sense of balance has to be applied to the struggle for political change. We need to proceed courageously, while remaining alert to all possible dangers and taking whatever steps may be necessary to minimise risk.

The threat of military invasion is highly unlikely. It's one thing for Western governments to launch air strikes against dictators in Baghdad or Belgrade; it would be a different matter entirely to attempt to militarily crush a democratically elected socialist government in Scotland.

Moreover, it is almost inconceivable that a socialist government could take power in Scotland except as part of a general upsurge of socialist radicalism across Europe and further afield. A victory for socialist change in Scotland would presuppose a seismic shift in the international balance of forces between Left and Right. Under these circumstances, governments in London, Brussels, and elsewhere would be more preoccupied with holding back the movement for socialism within their own backyards than with planning military adventures abroad.

But what of the danger of an internal backlash: a military coup, for example? After all, that's what happened in Chile in the 1970s. There, a democratically elected socialist government was overthrown in a brutal military takeover orchestrated behind the scenes by the American CIA and spearheaded by Margaret Thatcher's dear friend, General Augusto Pinochet. In the ensuing slaughter, tens of thousands of socialists, trade unionists, and human-rights activists were massacred.

Could the election of a socialist government in Scotland provoke such a savage reaction here? On the one hand, we should recognise that conditions in Europe at this stage are not exactly the same as in Latin America in the 1970s. In 1973, Chile was an island of democracy surrounded by military dictatorships. That was the normal form of government at that time in Latin America, and in parts of Europe too, including Spain, Portugal, and Greece. In Chile itself, although its parliamentary system had earned the country the nickname 'the Britain of Latin America', violence and repression against trade unionists and political dissidents had been commonplace throughout the 1950s and 1960s.

Even then, the Chilean generals were unable to launch an immediate coup against the left-wing government, which initially commanded the support of the rank and file of the armed forces and the police. Only three years on, after Chilean big business had brought the country to a state of chaos through prolonged economic sabotage, had the ground finally been prepared for the military junta to move in, with the support of the country's large middle class.[4]

In Chile, the right wing pro-CIA parties were able to muster 45 per cent of the vote even in the early days of the Allende government, when his popularity was at its height. In contrast, despite the decade-long retreat of socialism, the traditional right-wing party in Scotland, the Tory Party, has been reduced to just 15 per cent of the popular vote.

For all of these reasons, it would be much more difficult for the ruling establishment to use military force against an elected socialist government in Scotland. But neither should we be complacent. In 1993, Roy Hattersley, then deputy leader of the Labour Party, issued this sombre warning: 'Never underestimate the British establishment's ruthless determination to destroy its enemies.'[5] Another former deputy leader of the Labour Party, George Brown also explained, in one of his more lucid moments, that 'no privileged group disappears from the scene of history without a struggle and usually with no holds barred'.

A future socialist government in Scotland could cut across the threat of reaction by building and sustaining mass popular support at home and abroad. That means very swiftly taking full control over the direction of the economy to prevent disruption and destabilisation by big business. It means creating a dense network of democratic committees in every community, every workplace, every university, to involve hundreds of thousands of people in the task of transforming society. It also means generating support right across the world and building a new socialist international to unite the forces resisting capitalism internationally. This task has been made immeasurably easier by the evolution of the World Wide Web, a medium used to spectacular effect by the Zapatista movement in Mexico over the past five years. Many commentators believe that, without the Internet, the peasant guerrillas of Chiapas would possibly have been crushed long ago by the Mexican government.[6]

A socialist government would also need to protect itself by dismantling the old hierarchical power structures and replacing these with new democratic institutions. For example, instead of moving towards a national police force, as New Labour and Tory politicians advocate, a socialist government in Scotland would move in the opposite direction, towards a more locally based community police force, under the control of local councils.

The authoritarian command structure of the present armed forces would be dismantled. The army, navy, and air force are effectively run by an officer caste who were educated at exclusive fee-paying schools, who have spent their whole lives in the rarefied environment of the military establishment, and who are subject to no democratic accountability. The armed forces themselves mirror the class divide within society as a whole, with top generals earning six-figure salaries while ordinary squaddies are paid just £13,000, out of which they have to pay for accommodation and food.

A socialist Scotland would reconstruct new defence forces, which would be democratic, egalitarian, and accountable. Instead of defending the Establishment against the people, which is the ultimate function of the armed forces under capitalism, their primary role would be to defend democracy against internal and external sabotage.

Of course, introducing such radical changes would involve challenging centuries of tradition and standing up to powerful vested interests. At each step in the struggle to transform Scotland from a capitalist country into a socialist country, it will be necessary to win over a majority of the population by arguing out the case for change powerfully and convincingly.

It would be dishonest to pretend that the transition to socialism will be achieved next week or next month. It will be a protracted process involving hundreds upon hundreds of struggles and ruptures, during which the old order will be torn asunder. But the battles for the future of Scotland are more likely to be political, social and industrial battles rather than military battles. Socialist should also take great encouragement from the successful struggles against oppression that have been waged internationally over the past two decades. Since 1979, a rogues' gallery of American-backed dictators, including the Shah of Iran, Somosa in Nicaragua, Marcos in the Phillipines, and Suharto in Indonesia, have been toppled like traffic cones under the juggernaut of peaceful mass protest. In Eastern Europe too, mighty armies and feared secret police forces crumbled like sandcastles when mass mutiny erupted on the streets.

Although none of these revolutions led to the establishment of new socialist democracies, they all provided a glimpse of the real power that ordinary people possess when they act in unison. As the French writer Victor Hugo once declared, 'No army can withstand the strength of an idea whose time has come.'

Chapter Fifteen

A TIME TO TAKE SIDES

BACK IN THE 19th century, the Scottish historian Thomas Carlyle stated, 'History is the biography of great men.' Many of us remember being taught in school the story of Robert the Bruce and the spider. Or the story of Mary Queen of Scots who ended up getting her head chopped off. Or the story of Bonnie Prince Charlie arriving on a boat in the West Highlands to proclaim the Jacobite Rebellion.

These are certainly colourful tales. Stories of the exploits of heroic individuals such as William Wallace, or the legendary Clydeside revolutionary socialist John Maclean, undoubtedly help to bring history to life.

But the history lessons, the historical novels, and the Hollywood blockbusters invariably fail to recognise the role that ordinary people play in shaping events. History is not made primarily by charismatic individuals, it is made by the masses.

The history of the past two centuries is an epic story of exploitation, injustice, war, greed, and treachery. But it is also a heroic tale of resistance, defiance, solidarity, selflessness, and sacrifice by millions of ordinary people.

Here in Scotland, key landmarks in the past 200 years of struggle have included the 1820 weavers' insurrection; the Chartist uprising; the Highland Land League battles against the tyranny of the landlords; the Glasgow rent strikes of 1915; the campaign of the Suffragettes; the workers' revolt that earned the West of Scotland the nickname 'Red Clydeside'; the 'People's Republic of Fife', when miners took control of their pit villages during the 1926 General Strike; the giant protest marches and the decades of direct action against nuclear weapons; the UCS work-in; the year-long miners' strike of 1984–85; the Poll Tax mass non-payment campaign which led to the toppling of Thatcher; and the defeat of the Tory plans to privatise Scottish water.

There have also been countless, more localised, workplace, community, and environmental struggles against exploitation and injustice. In recent years, these have included occupations of closure-threatened schools and community centres in Glasgow; occupations of factories such as Caterpillar in Lanarkshire and Glacier Metal in Glasgow; illegal defiance demos in Glasgow and Edinburgh against the Tory Criminal Justice Act; and environmental battles against motorway construction projects, genetically-modified crops, toxic-waste dumps, nuclear weapons, nuclear dumping, and opencast mines.

Some of these struggles were successful; others were lost. But all of them, individually and combined, had a profound impact on those who participated in them and upon society as a whole. Without these battles against injustice, life today would be more primitive, more barren, more oppressive.

But what has all this to do with socialism? After all, these weren't really movements to change society; they were movements to improve society, to reform society.

It has plenty to with to socialism for two reasons. First, because this never-ending treadmill of conflict can only be halted by the creation of a new society. The heroism, the energy, the talent that has been devoured by struggle over the ages could have and should have been channelled more creatively. But capitalism by its nature forces people to fight ferociously for the most meagre reforms. Like Sisyphus, the character in Greek mythology who had to keep rolling the stone up to the top of the hill, working-class people have had to keep battling, generation after generation, sometimes even just to stand still.

Secondly, because whenever people take action against their employer, or against the government, or against a private company that is desecrating their local environment, they get a taste of their own power.

We are brought up in a culture of deference. Politics is not for ordinary people, but for an educated elite. Yes, you're allowed to trudge out to the polling station every few years to send some middle-class pin-striped social climber to Westminster or Holyrood. But in between times you're expected to entertain yourself with soap operas, football, and pop music, while the politicians get on with the important business of making sure that the rich keep on getting richer.

Whenever people participate in acts of resistance, they begin to change. They begin to see things more clearly. They begin to understand more thoroughly how society works. They begin to feel more confident about themselves and less confident in the politicians and businessmen. They begin to question all the old prejudices, all the old attitudes, all the old certainties that they've always accepted as gospel. In other words, the seeds of socialism are sown in struggle.

Before the Poll Tax was introduced, people had begun to believe that the then Tory Prime Minister, Margaret Thatcher, was invincible. She had seen off the miners, the railworkers, the printworkers, the nurses. It seemed to some people that nothing, but nothing, could be done to stop her. That was the unspoken belief that paralysed the trade union and labour movement in the 1980s.

The Labour leader at the time, Neil Kinnock, condemned those organising against the Poll Tax in the most venomous language. They were, he said, 'Toytown revolutionaries who pretend the tax can be stopped and the government toppled by mass non-payment.'[1] Within a year of Kinnock's outburst, the tax *was* stopped, and the head of the government *was* toppled, by mass non-payment.

The defeat of the Poll Tax did not just remove a hated tax which blatantly discriminated against the poor. It also changed people's attitudes towards the law and those who administer it. Particularly in working-class areas, the culture of deference to authority was torn down and has never been re-established.

As the song says, 'Freedom's just another word for nothing left to lose.' The battle for socialism won't be spearheaded by prosperous politicians or middle-class intellectuals but by those who have nothing to lose and everything to gain from the defeat of capitalism. Working-class women, especially, will be in the front line.

Socialism is not an exclusive club. The building of a new society can never be achieved by a minority, no matter how far-sighted, heroic or self-sacrificing that minority is. Socialism won't be achieved by a coup or a conspiracy. It won't be achieved by a group of politicians smuggling it in through a parliament, behind the backs of the population.

It will only be feasible when the mass of the population of Scotland, or of any other country, decides to take matters into its own hands. Passive support is not enough; like a house, socialism has to be built from the bottom up rather than from the top down.

Electing dedicated socialist politicians who are prepared to live the same lifestyle as ordinary working people is an important part of the battle to change society. But it is not enough. Unfortunately, the battle for the future of society won't unfold like a game of cricket on the village green. The parasitic elite at the top of society will stop at nothing to protect their power and privileges. They will whip up hysteria. They will seek to suppress opposition.

But the working class in Scotland, which includes manual workers, white-collar workers, professional workers, pensioners, lone parents, and students, constitutes a mighty force.

Over 90 per cent of Scots have an income below £30,000 a year. 75 per cent have an income of less than £20,000 a year. By contrast, less than half of one per cent of Scots earned more than £90,000 a year.[2]

These raw figures expose the real balance of forces between the rich and the rest. As the 19th-century English revolutionary poet Percy Bysshe Shelley declared in his inspiring poem, 'The Mask of Anarchy', 'We are many, ye are few.'

Even now, there is a growing gulf between, on the one side, the businessmen who run the country and politicians who think they run the country, and, on the other side, the people.

In late 1998, the findings of an extensive opinion survey were published in a newspaper. People were asked if they backed 'higher taxes to provide better public services'; 73 per cent said yes. They were asked if they agreed with the statement that 'there is one law for the rich and another for the poor'; 74 per cent said yes. They were asked whether 'trade unions should have more of a say in the running of industry and the economy'; 51 per cent said yes.

Perhaps the most significant finding of all, given the sustained ideological onslaught that has been waged for the last ten years against the idea of socialism: 43 per cent of Scots agreed with the statement that 'there should be more socialist planning'.

This was not a poll commissioned by the *Scottish Socialist Voice* or some other left-wing newspaper. It was not even commissioned by *The Scotsman*, which published the findings. It was conducted by the ICM polling organisation on behalf of . . . the Scottish Conservative Party![3]

Others polls, including a recent Scottish Social Attitudes Survey, have shown huge majorities in favour of measures such as redistribution of wealth from the rich to the poor and the bringing back into public ownership of the privatised utilities and rail companies.

The double-barrelled devolution referendum in 1997 confounded many media commentators. They expected a majority Yes on the first question, which asked whether people agreed with the principle of a Scottish Parliament. But equally, they expected a No vote on the second question, which asked whether people wanted that parliament to have tax-raising powers. Journalists claimed that no electorate anywhere in the world had ever voted in favour of a general tax-raising mandate.

'If Scotland votes Yes on the second question they will have gone where no modern electorate has gone before – and upset one of the laws of contemporary political behaviour,' wrote one *Scotsman* commentator on the eve of the referendum. The next day, in a resounding rejection of the values of private greed over public need, the electorate voted by a two-to-one majority to go 'where none had gone before'.

Not one of Scotland's four traditional political parties would dare to promote such seditious policies as wealth redistribution, workers' management or public ownership. Nor would any of Scotland's mass circulation newspapers, TV stations, or radio stations ever give any credence to such fanatical extremism.

Yet these are mainstream ideas held by millions of ordinary people from all walks of life in Scotland today. Following a recent BBC *Question Time* programme filmed in Glasgow, the editor-in-chief of *The Scotsman*, Andrew Neil, could scarcely contain his rage at the left-wing attitudes expressed by the audience. 'I have been around long enough to know that a Glasgow audience will be more left-wing than most,' he fulminated. But this was 'beyond the pale of mainstream politics even for Scotland . . . Throughout the programme not one voice spoke up for the market economy.'[4]

Those who live and work among real people in Scotland don't have to watch *Question Time* to discover that the popularity of the market economy is a cosy myth dreamed up by newspaper moguls with six-figure salaries. What's more, the ideas of socialism – of social equality, of people before profit, of open democracy rather than closed hierarchy – are growing in popularity, not just in Scotland but across the world.

In a fitting farewell to the last century, 100,000 people marched in Seattle, one of the richest cities in the world, against the world's business and political elite. This was one of the biggest protest demos seen in the United States since the outpouring of rage against the Vietnam War in the 1960s. But what set the 'Battle of Seattle' apart from the thousands upon thousands of other protest actions of the last 50 years was its purpose. This was no single-issue movement, focusing on a specific injustice; this was a protest directed at the entire global capitalist system.

Since then, other similar actions have been organised in cities across the world. Protests, not just against poverty, not just against the destruction of the environment, not just against unemployment; but protests against all of these things, and against capitalism itself.

This is of immense significance. When resistance to capitalism is divided into different fragments labelled 'animal-rights protest', 'trade-union protest', 'anti-road protest', 'anti-nuclear protest', each can be picked off and defeated, just as the individual strands of a rope can easily be snapped. But when the protests are woven together, like the strands of a rope, they become stronger and less easily broken.

Veteran socialist firebrand Tony Benn used to observe that at left-wing demos and conferences, people would wear badges against the bomb, badges against low pay, badges against racism.

'But when will people start wearing badges against capitalism?' he asked. By the start of this century, more and more people across the globe were prepared to define themselves as 'anti-capitalist'. That's an important start, but it is only a start. We can oppose, resist, defy, obstruct, challenge, rebel against the system. But time and time again, the question will arise: 'What is your alternative?'

The battle against capitalism is not just about action; it is also about ideology. It is about constructing an alternative vision that will inspire people to sweep aside all obstacles in order to turn that vision into reality. That doesn't mean that we just preach the gospel of socialism and ask people to wait for the promised land. Socialists don't just prepare for the future; we participate in the present.

Right now, socialists are fighting for the Scottish Parliament to redistribute wealth and income by introducing a new fairer form of local taxation based on ability to pay. Even though Holyrood has only limited powers, it could nonetheless scrap the Council Tax and introduce a Scottish Service Tax within two years, effectively raising the top rate of taxation in Scotland from 40 per cent to 52 per cent, and sharing this money out among low-income households. This would not eradicate poverty and inequality in Scotland. But, set against the last two decades of wealth redistribution from the poor to the rich, it would mark a turning of the tide. It would in all likelihood pave the way for further struggles, further changes, and further victories in the future.

Genuine socialists will always fight for reforms, for improvements, no matter how modest, in the lives of ordinary people. Those who stand aloof from the day-to-day struggle against oppression and exploitation will never gain the credibility to help shape the future. But one thing that differentiates conscious socialism from militant trade unionism, or from radical environmentalism, is that we have a clear goal, a definite destination. To reach that destination, we need audacity, but we also need clarity; we need courage, but we also need knowledge; we need conviction, but we also need vision.

Part Four

IMAGINE

You may say I'm a dreamer
But I'm not the only one
I hope some day you'll join us
And the world will live as one.

Chapter Sixteen

UNDER NEW MANAGEMENT

IN 1971, INSPIRED by the UCS work-in, when thousands of Clydeside shipbuilders seized control of their yards, John Lennon wrote a number-one hit, 'Power to the People'. One of the central tasks of socialism in the 21st century will be to bring that stirring slogan to life.

Socialism is not just about redistribution of wealth; it is also about redistribution of power. One of the first tasks of a socialist government would be to carry out a wholesale democratic transformation of society at local, national, and, eventually, international level.

Under capitalism, a powerful minority dictate to the majority. Ordinary people have no real say in how society is run. All the key decisions that affect our everyday lives – about our work, our environment, our health, our children's education, our food, our public transport, our housing – are taken behind closed doors by tight-knit cliques of faceless bureaucrats and wealthy businessmen.

Every year, a large-scale survey of public attitudes throughout the UK is undertaken by the National Council for Social Research. In 1999, the survey found that 80 per cent of people believed that the income gap between rich and poor was too wide; 73 per cent believed that it was the government's responsibility to narrow that gap; 66 per cent of people said they wanted higher spending on health, education, and welfare, even if that meant paying higher taxes; 70 per cent said that congestion in cities was a serious problem; and 93 per cent wanted an improvement in public transport.[1]

Other surveys conducted specifically in Scotland have shown massive support for a repeal of anti-trade-union legislation, for the closure of the nuclear bases on the Clyde, and for increased welfare and unemployment benefits.

If we lived in a real democracy which reflected people's views, wealth would be redistributed from rich to poor. There would be vast increases in health, education, and welfare spending. Big resources would be ploughed into public transport to reduce congestion and pollution. Thatcher's anti-trade-union legislation would be repealed. Instead of a relentless witch-hunt against the unemployed, benefits would be increased.

These are the things that the public want. But they get the opposite. Over the past 25 years, there have been five general elections and five different Prime Ministers in office – three Labour and two Tory. Yet, through all of these changes, the rich have grown richer and the poor poorer; spending on health, education, and welfare has been slashed; public transport has deteriorated; trade-union activity is more rigidly repressed in the UK than in any other state in Western Europe; unemployment benefits, pensions, and other state benefits have diminished.

Imagine you're a pensioner lying at home suffering from an illness. You ask a neighbour to go to the shop and bring you back a loaf, a pint of milk, and a dozen eggs. Instead, she comes back with a tin of dog food, a bottle of sauce, and a tin of shoe polish and says: 'I've brought you back these things instead, because I decided that's what you really wanted.'

That's roughly how British parliamentary democracy works in practice. There are some differences of course. For example, while you can ask a different neighbour to do your shopping the next time, you can't get rid of a politician quite so easily. And, of course, unlike your neighbour, the politicians who ignore your instructions don't do it voluntarily, they're paid lavish sums of money to misrepresent you.

Parliamentary democracy is a very limited and partial form of democracy. It leads to passivity by encouraging people to 'leave politics to the politicians', rather than take control of their own lives. It is elitist because it creates a separate class of professional politicians who see themselves as more qualified, more intellectually equipped, more sophisticated than the broad mass of the population.

A 40-year-old in Scotland today will have had the opportunity to vote in just five general elections. If they live in a rock-solid Labour seat, as most Scots do, and vote for one of the other parties, their five votes will effectively have been wasted. Even if they did vote Labour, their vote would have made no difference to the outcome of any of these five elections.

To make matters worse, people in Scotland can vote overwhelmingly in one direction, and end up with a government that few people voted for. That's what happened in four of the five general elections in which today's 40-year-olds had the opportunity to participate; and that's what will happen again and again in many future general elections until Scotland has its own independent parliament.

The right to vote is a basic human right which all socialists would defend to the death. But all elections should be conducted democratically, through proportional representation and on a level playing field, with, for example, equal access for all parties to the media. There is also an overwhelming case for annually elected parliaments and councils to ensure that the politicians are accountable to the people, not just once every four or five years, but constantly.

Nor should voting be condensed into a single day. Instead of a polling *day*, there should be a polling *week*, to ensure that everyone who wants to vote is able to do so. Socialists also advocate the right to vote at 16. It is outrageous that a 16-year-old who works for a living, and is perhaps even married with a family, should be denied the right to vote.

In a future socialist society, parliamentary representatives would no longer be a privileged elite with salaries and lifestyles way above the people they are supposed to represent. Instead they'd be paid the average salary of a skilled worker.

Even so, parliaments, whether located in Edinburgh or in London, are not the be-all and end-all of democracy. Serbia, for example, has a parliament complete with opposition parties. But a parliament does not signify genuine democracy any more than a paintbrush signifies a genuine work of art.

Socialism is about extending democracy to allow everyone to participate in the key decisions that affect their lives, their communities, and their nations. Socialism is about moving away from *representative* democracy – in which other people take all the important decisions on your behalf – towards *direct* democracy.

The whole of capitalist society is based on top-down hierarchical structures which rule through fear and favouritism, bullying and patronage. Those who conform are rewarded with promotion, while those who express dissent are banished into the wilderness. As a result, mediocrity rises to the top, while talent, originality, and creativity is stifled.

The whole system is lubricated with money. In a diverse range of organisations, from business corporations to trade unions, from local quangos to national governments, the higher you rise in the hierarchy, the greater your financial rewards. Under capitalism, it pays to be subservient to your superiors.

Socialism, by contrast, is about creating grassroots democracy from the bottom upwards. In a genuine socialist system, there could be mass decision-making on all the big issues through democratic referenda. There could also be maximum decentralisation of power right down to local communities and workplaces. And, in place of the unelected bureaucracies and hand-picked quangos that run whole areas of our lives under capitalism, there could be new administrative bodies which would be elected and subject to democratic control.

The idea of such a far-reaching democratic transformation of society will be bitterly opposed by the power structures that control our lives today. 'You can't have real democracy,' claim the politicians and bureaucrats. 'It's utopian. It's impractical. And in any case, we know best. Only we have the expertise required to take all these complicated decisions.' In industry and commerce, top managers and executives are equally vehement in their opposition to workplace democracy. Any measure of workers control would result in chaos, they insist.

The idea that the broad mass of people are too ignorant or too stupid to take important decisions is deeply rooted in the class system. Back in the 1830s, the Chartist demand for universal suffrage was opposed unanimously by the rich and powerful. One of their main arguments was that it would lead to 'mob rule'. The famous historian, Thomas Macaulay, thundered against the preposterous idea that the lower orders should have the right to vote, claiming that it would 'lead to the destruction of civilisation and a return to barbarism'. Even the reformist philosopher, John Stuart Mill, made the point: 'We dreaded the ignorance and especially the selfishness and brutality of the masses.'

A century and a half later, people look back in bewilderment at the idea that only people with property could be considered sufficiently responsible to have the right to vote. In the future, people will be equally bewildered at the lack of democracy in society today, where the mass of the population are excluded from real decision-making for exactly the same reasons that their ancestors were excluded from voting in the 19th century.

Why should key decisions that affect a community be taken

by people who are not even part of that community? Why should politicians or council executives have the power to close down a school, a library, or a community centre without the permission of the local community? Why should government officials be entitled to bulldoze a motorway through a village or an urban neighbourhood without even consulting the people whose lives will be turned upside down by that decision?

On a national scale, why should the people of Scotland, without consultation, be forced to endure the existence of the largest nuclear arsenal in Europe barely 20 miles from the centre of Glasgow? Why should governments be allowed to sell off public assets at bargain basement prices to jumped-up Del Boys when most people want these assets to remain public property?

Unfortunately, even some people on the Left fear democracy. They lack confidence that their ideas will hold sway. They oppose referendums and secret ballots because they fear that they will lose the vote. Their paternalistic vision of socialism is based on the idea that it's possible for an enlightened minority to impose progressive beliefs and values on everyone else. But the road to hell is paved with good intentions. Without grassroots democracy, in which the people as a whole have the ultimate say over the running of society, the result will be bureaucratism, oppression, and dictatorship.

Some people genuinely, but mistakenly, fear that any expansion of democracy would simply transfer more influence to the press tycoons. They argue that, whenever a referendum was called, mass-circulation newspapers like the *Sun* and the *Daily Record* would be able to sway public opinion in line with there own vested interests and the personal prejudices of their owners. Professional politicians, by contrast, are supposed to be immune from such pressures.

It is a mystery why anyone should imagine that political leaders are less easily manipulated than the general public. Rupert

Murdoch, for example, owner of the *Sun, The Times, The Sunday Times* and BskyB, had the last three prime ministers of the UK in his back pocket – even though he is an American citizen and pays not a penny in taxes to the British exchequer.

Most people go about their daily working lives without a moment's thought as to whether the editor of the *Sun*, or the *Daily Record* or the *Daily Mail* approves of what they're doing. But not our top political leaders. Every move they make is influenced by what they think the press might say. Most ordinary mortals, by contrast, have a healthy scepticism towards the press, and certainly don't spend a large part of then lives worrying about the next editorial in the *Daily Express*.

In any case, a socialist government would stand up to the media moguls and ensure that the future battle of ideas will be fought out on a level battleground. In a socialist society, minority and alternative newspapers, magazines, and radio and TV stations would be granted equal access to the most advanced printing, digital, and broadcasting technology. Distribution networks that are today monopolised by the giant media corporations could be opened up to everyone. There would be the flourishing of a genuinely free and diverse press and media which are not under the thumb of big business advertisers. At the same time, there could be an expansion of community and socially owned media organs, providing equal access to all shades of opinion on any contentious issues that arose.

The ruling classes will, of course, throw up all sorts of arguments against direct democracy. Like their great-grandfathers before them, they fear that the great unruly mob out there can never be trusted with real democracy. They'll claim that it's not practical. They'll argue that it would be too time-consuming. They'll maintain that it would be too costly to administer annual elections, repeated referenda, and new democratic administrative structures.

Ten years ago, such objections would have been at least partly valid. But the advance of technology has opened the door to a gigantic democratic leap forward. Even Tony Blair has promised that every household in the UK will be online within five years. Some experts have slammed Blair as too cautious and have argued that every household could be online within just two years. Direct democracy via electronic voting and online referenda is no longer the stuff of science fiction.

A socialist constitution could enshrine the right of people to organise petitions to demand a referendum on any local, regional, or national issue. As a safeguard, to prevent frivolous abuse of the new democratic constitution, a minimum number of signatures, based on a fixed percentage of the electorate, would be required to trigger a referendum.

Of course, only the big decisions would require nationwide referenda. Numerous day-to-day decisions have to be taken in any society. These routine decisions could naturally be delegated to managers and administrators. But, rather than being run from above by a top-down hierarchy, a future socialist democracy would be run from the grassroots upwards, with executives and managers fully accountable to those they serve.

Workplaces could be democratically run, with elected workers' councils established in every sizeable workplace to ratify key decisions on wages, working conditions, the hiring and firing of labour, production targets, and investment. These workplace councils could in turn send delegates to industry-wide councils to formulate, in conjunction with the elected government and consumer groups a more general plan for the industry as a whole.

All anti-trade-union laws would be repealed. Trade unions would be completely free from all government interference. A free and independent trade-union movement will always be a necessary counterweight against abuse and exploitation, even in a democratic socialist state. The trade-union movement itself is certain to be transformed along more democratic lines in the course of the struggle for socialism, with the leadership fully under the control of the membership, and receiving broadly the same incomes as the workers they represent.

In a socialist Scotland, local democracy too will be vital. The existing network of community councils could be delegated far greater powers, including control over local budgets. A host of decisions that are today taken by officials who have no local knowledge could be devolved right down to neighbourhood level. Community councils, along with tenants and residents associations, could arbitrate over complaints of antisocial behaviour, take control over local policing, decide on any necessary traffic-calming measures, run local-community facilities, deal with housing allocations, and generally act as a community government accountable to local people.

Inevitably, there would be problems and conflicts, especially in the early days of socialist change. But that's no reason for inertia. Whatever the difficulties involved in developing genuine grassroots democracy, these would be more than cancelled out by the dynamism and energy that could be unleashed by the involvement of hundreds of thousands of people across Scotland in the running of their communities and workplaces.

'But this is a recipe for anarchy,' the rich and powerful will no doubt object. 'It's utopian, it's unworkable, it would lead to mayhem.' For the ruling Establishment, the debate over the running of society is a game of 'heads we win, tales you lose'. On the one hand, they try to whip up fear and suspicion by claiming that socialism would mean a centralised state bureaucracy dictating every detail of people's lives. But then, on the other hand, they insist that democratic libertarian socialism – the polar opposite of bureaucratic Stalinism – is unworkable. This is, of course, very convenient, because it means that there is no alternative but to preserve the status quo. Fortunately, it doesn't stand up to serious scrutiny.

It is true that no genuine socialist democracy has ever yet been established. But there have been enough tantalising glimpses of socialist democracy in action to prove its viability. For example, in Catalonia, in 1936–37, ordinary working people took over agriculture and industry and reorganised society along democratic lines. Railways, buses, shipping, gas and electricity-generating stations, textile mills, mines, car and engineering factories, food-processing plants, breweries, newspapers, department stores, hotels, bars, and restaurants were taken over by their workers and run on democratic lines.

In those heady days of revolution, even though there was a war against fascism raging across the whole of Spain, production hugely increased in Catalonia, allowing wages and living standards to rise. On the Barcelona trams, the number of passenger journeys rose by one million a week over the course of a year. The number of trams and services increased, fares were lowered, wages raised, and safety increased. During this time, the entire tramway network was run by the tramway workers themselves through mass meetings and democratically elected committees.[2]

In May 1968, in France, when students and workers brought the government to its knees in a revolutionary challenge to the old order, creative democracy flourished gloriously for a short period.

In Paris, neighbourhood committees of action sprang up and took over responsibility for local services and transport. In Nantes, the entire city was run directly by the people for a brief period. Working-class women in the city, together with local farmers, set up co-operative food outlets, cutting out the retail giants, and slashed prices.

Over 12,000 striking broadcast workers drew up alternative plans for the running of TV and radio. They proposed that all news coverage should be impartial, that there should be no government interference or pressure on broadcasters, and that political parties should have access to TV and radio proportionate to their support. Health workers drew up plans to reorganise hospitals along democratic lines. Even footballers took over the headquarters of the French Football Federation and demanded the democratisation of the game.[3]

Nearer home, a whole series of workplace and community struggles have provided living breathing testimony to the effectiveness of socialist democracy. In the early 1970s, faced with mass redundancies, thousands of shipyard workers took over the order books and ran four Clydeside shipyards for over a year. All the key decisions were taken at mass meetings of the entire workforce, while an elected co-ordinating committee dealt with the day-to-day running of the campaign.

Without anything like the resources that today's charity extravaganzas are able to command, the Clydeside workers raised a phenomenal half a million pounds — the equivalent of around £10 million in today's money. They also built international support for the campaign to the point where, right across the world, the initials UCS came to symbolise working-class resistance against social injustice, and working-class power in action.[4]

Fifteen years later, during the Caterpillar factory occupation in Lanarkshire, the workforce again carried on production after the factory had officially closed. Despite the lack of available materials, they managed to produce a huge earth-moving tractor, which they painted pink to distinguish it from Caterpillar products, which were painted in corporate bright yellow. Dubbed the Pink Panther, the workers' tractor was donated to Live Aid and transported to Africa to assist the fight against famine.[5]

Today, in hundreds of communities across Scotland, thousands of voluntary and non-profit organisations from residents' associations to bowling clubs, from parent-and-toddler groups to pensioners' clubs operate efficiently without hierarchies, shareholders, or managing directors.

The Jack Jardine Memorial Hall in Glasgow's Pollok housing scheme is an instructive example of community democracy in action. In 1997, this community facility, then called the Ladymuir Centre, was closed down by Glasgow City Council.

It had run clubs for the elderly. Bingo sessions, children's discos, drama classes, dance classes had all been on offer. It had provided after-school care projects and college-tutored courses. It had been a focal point for young people who would gather in the centre to play pool, learn the guitar, or have a coffee and a chat.

When the closure was announced, the community sprang into action. They occupied the hall and elected a committee to take over the day-to-day running of the centre. The electricity was cut off by the council. So too were the telephones. There was no funding to buy equipment or to employ staff.

Yet, for three long years, local people battled on against all the odds to preserve this oasis of hope in a blighted deprived housing scheme. They were threatened with legal action, but carried on regardless. They raised cash. They acquired equipment. They organised gala days, fireworks displays, pensioners outings. Despite having to climb over mountain ranges of obstacles, such as the disconnection of electricity, they continued to provide activities such as bingo, band practice, yoga, sewing classes, children's parties, a youth club.

They opened the doors of the hall to everyone in the community. After the three years, the authorities were forced to concede defeat and recognise that the centre should stay open under the control of the local community.

The legendary football manager, Bill Shankly, once described the co-operation and teamwork of a football team in action as a form of socialism. The Jack Jardine Memorial Hall, renamed after one of the late stalwarts of the campaign, is also a form of socialism in action, and provides a glimpse of the type of society we could build by harnessing the skills, talents, and energy of millions of ordinary people.

These examples are not exact blueprints for a future socialist democracy. But they do provide a glimmer of insight into the talent, the flair, and the organisational skills that ordinary people possess. That energy and creativity is stifled and suppressed by the hierarchical social structures of capitalism.

These antiquated structures may have served a purpose once upon a time. But in this new hi-tech century, they are becoming as obsolete as the feudal structures they replaced. Elitism, authoritarianism, hierarchy, and bureaucracy have had their day. Some time in the course of this century – and the sooner the better – they will be swept away and replaced with egalitarian democracy. As Bob Dylan sang, 'Your old road is rapidly ageing.'

Chapter Seventeen

THE GROWLING MONGREL

SOCIALISM IS AN internationalist philosophy. (In the words of the song, 'Imagine there's no countries, I wonder if you can; nothing to kill or die for, a brotherhood of man.'

Some time in the future these words will be turned into reality. The resources of the world will become common international property. People will look back in horror to the days when the world was divided into hundreds of warring tribes, each armed to the teeth with tanks, machine guns, battleships, and fighter aeroplanes. Future generations will be incredulous at the very notion of scientists and technicians spending their lives designing and refining weapons capable of reducing the whole planet to dust. They will look back in astonishment to the dawn of the 21st century, when the people of one rich country consumed 50 times as much food per head as the people of one poor country. And they will scarcely believe the historians when they describe how the planet itself was almost obliterated from the solar system to satisfy the insatiable greed of a small minority.) _ GOOD QUOTE FOR WEBSITE?

Back in the 1840s, the socialist philosophers, Karl Marx and Friedrich Engels, first raised the idea of a socialist world. In the days before cars, telephones, and radios had even been invented, such a vision required a phenomenal historical imagination. But in the age of the Internet, high-speed air travel, instantaneous global communications, satellite TV, and global capitalism, the idea of global socialism can no longer be dismissed as a flight of poetic fantasy.

So where do we begin? How do we get from here to there? How could a lone parent in Dundee, a nurse in Glasgow or a factory worker in Fife possibly participate in such a colossal enterprise as building worldwide socialism?

The fact is, the struggle to transform the planet we live on is as much a local struggle as it is a global struggle. Worldwide socialism will not be achieved in one broad sweep; it will be the final product of multiple movements against capitalism at community, regional, and national level.

The spread of genuine socialism in the future will be just as contagious as the pro-democracy movement which engulfed Eastern Europe in 1989–90. A series of local demonstrations in the East German city of Leipzig in late 1989 rapidly spread right across the country, then expanded outwards into neighbouring states. Within a few months, every Stalinist regime in Eastern Europe had collapsed. Although the story had no happy ending, it nonetheless demonstrated the lightning speed at which events can reverberate across international borders.

The struggle for socialism is unlikely to erupt simultaneously across the globe. Nor will it unfold evenly and uniformly. Because of differing national traditions and conditions, any future movement against capitalism is likely to evolve in a fragmented and disjointed fashion, with events in one country spreading rapidly across international borders.

There is an important socialist dimension to the national question in Scotland today, and an important national dimension to the struggle for socialism. Many people support the idea of independence, not because they are parochial nationalists or anti-English bigots, but because they want greater control over their own lives and want to move towards a more egalitarian society.

It is no accident that those most strongly in favour of an

independent Scotland are young people and working-class people. In general, the people who want radical constitutional change are the same people who want radical social change. For a growing number of people in Scotland, the break-up of the British state means striking out in a revolutionary direction and burying the past.

Neither is it a coincidence that big business, with the exception of one or two isolated mavericks, is bitterly hostile towards the idea of independence. After more than two decades of Thatcherism — first under Thatcher, then under Major, and now under Blair — the United Kingdom has been transformed into a free-market paradise with some of the highest profit levels, the lowest wages, and the most repressive anti-trade-union laws in the western world.

The cringeing unionism of Scotland's bankers, landowners and wealthy businessmen conforms to a historical pattern stretching back 1000 years. Over and over again, almost from time immemorial, Scotland's ruling classes have worked with the English ruling classes to suppress dissent.

Scotland is one of the oldest nations in Europe. As far back as the 13th century, the beginning of a national consciousness was forged during the struggle against the forcible incorporation of Scotland into Edward the First's fendal kingdom. Under his reign of terror over Scotland, 2000 members of the Scottish nobility — earls, barons, and bishops — signed the oath of allegiance to the English king. It was left to an outlaw, William Wallace, and his co-leader, Andrew Murray, to organise a mass movement of resistance. Their ragged guerrilla armies were made up of the landless peasantry, the craftsmen, the dispossessed nobility, and the poor.

In contradiction of the mythology propagated by right-wing groups in America, who elevated the film *Braveheart* into a celebration of Celtic national-racial purity, Wallace's army included

Irish, French, Flemish, and English immigrants and united Gaelic-speaking Highlanders and English-speaking Lowland Scots.

Only after Wallace had swept through Scotland did the nobility eventually switch sides. Even then, their support for an independent Scotland was half-hearted and unreliable. Although Wallace was eventually defeated and tortured to death, his campaign set Scotland ablaze. The Wars of Independence raged on for the next 30 years, culminating in the victory of Robert the Bruce at the Battle of Bannockburn.

As a result, Scotland became an independent kingdom, while Wales and Ireland were held in chains as colonial possessions of the English aristocracy. The victory at Bannockburn enabled Scotland to evolve independently into a rudimentary nation-state with its own native ruling class and its own separate national economy.

But by the end of the 17th century, particularly as a result of the disastrous 'Darien Scheme', a vain attempt to compete with English and Spanish imperialism by establishing a colony in Central America, the Scottish ruling class had almost bankrupted the country. The bankers, landowners, and merchants began to turn to England for economic salvation.

After months of debate, the elite Scottish Parliament, elected by just 4000 people, backed the Act of Union. In effect, they sold Scottish independence for £400,000 cash, plus lucrative personal bribes and posts in the new British administration. The writer, Daniel Defoe, working in Edinburgh as an agent of the English government, wrote, 'The great men are posting to London for places and honours . . . I never saw so much trick, sham, pride, jealousy and cutting of friends' throats as there is among the noblemen. In short, money will do anything here.'[1]

Later, Robert Burns wrote:

'What force or guile could not subdue
Thro' many warlike ages
Is wrought now by a coward few
For hireling traitor's wages
The English steel we could disdain
Secure in valour's station
But English gold has been our bane
Sic' a parcel of rogues in a nation.'[2]

This was no federal union of two sovereign states. The English ruling class was not interested in forming an equal partnership or union with Scotland. Although allowed to retain its own church, its own legal system and its own education system, Scotland was stripped of all political and economic autonomy.

Outside parliament, Scotland was in uproar. English troops were moved to the border ready to mount an invasion as riots swept Edinburgh and Glasgow in protest at the decision to dissolve the Scottish Parliament. One English government agent in Edinburgh estimated the mood in Scotland at around 50 to 1 against the Union.[3]

Discontent with the union continued to fester for decades. By promising to restore the Scottish Parliament, Charles Edward Stuart, a French Catholic, built mass support in the Highlands and passive support even in the Presbyterian Lowlands as he launched his bid for the British throne in 1745. The Jacobite Rebellion was only routed after 'Bonnie Prince Charlie' marched into England. Later, with the rise and rise of the British Empire, Scotland's ruling classes started to turn more and more anglified. During the 19th century, they even began to drop the term 'Scotland' completely, preferring to describe themselves as 'North British'.

By contrast, within radical circles and especially in the emerging Labour movement, there remained a powerful yearning for Home Rule. This reflected the existence of an anti-imperialist sentiment and an affinity with Ireland and other oppressed nations of the British Empire.

In 1820, the Scottish Insurrection led by the weavers under the slogan 'Scotland: Free or a Desert', demanded universal suffrage and Scottish independence.[4] Keir Hardie's Scottish Labour Party, formed in 1888, included the demand for Home Rule as the fifth point in an 18-point programme. The Scottish TUC, formed as a radical breakaway from the British TUC in 1897, adopted a pro-Home Rule policy in 1914. Eight years later, when ten Independent Labour MPs were elected from Clydeside to Westminster, their first act was to present a Bill to the House of Commons calling for Scottish Home Rule.

Around the same period, the heroic Clydeside socialist, John MacLean, called for an independent Scottish socialist republic. In many ways, MacLean was a visionary, decades ahead of his time. In the early 1920s, MacLean's tiny Scottish Workers' Republican Party was the only pro-independence party in existence.[5] The SNP was not even formed until more than decade after MacLean's death and even then remained a marginal force in Scottish politics, with less than one per cent support for the first 25 years of its existence.[6]

Today unionism in Scotland is fighting a rearguard action. The closing decades of the 20th century witnessed a clear long-term trend towards the break-up of the United Kingdom and the creation of an independent Scotland.

It is a paradox of our times that in the age of global capitalism, when the ruling powers of the planet seek desperately to break down national boundaries and form huge trading blocs such as the European Union, the impulse from below is in the opposite direction.

The rise of nationalism internationally is a contradictory phenomenon. The fuel that drives the engine of national discontent is a complex mixture of emotions, grievances, prejudices, aspirations, and ideals. Some of these sentiments are reactionary, xenophobic, and parochial. Others are saturated with the spirit of democracy and justice. For many people, especially in small stateless nations such as Scotland, Wales, and the Basque Country, national identity is linked with opposition to centralism, regimentation, and uniformity.

In any nationalist movement, progressive and reactionary ideas invariably exist side by side. In some parts of the world, the character of nationalism is predominantly aggressive, tribalistic, and inward-looking. In the Balkans, nationalism has led to the tearing apart of integrated communities, ethnic cleansing, and rivers of blood as violent conflict rages over disputed territories.

That is not the case in Scotland, where the demand for national independence is about opposing nuclear weapons, standing against inequality, and prioritising public services over private greed. Contrary to unionist mythology, pro-independence sentiment and anti-English bigotry are two entirely different phenomena. Of course, there are Scottish nationalists who are bitterly anglophobic. But there are also plenty of tartan-clad rugby fans who will cheerfully belt out anti-English anthems at Murrayfield and then go to the ballot box and vote for the staunchly pro-union Tory Party. There are multitudes of football fans who work themselves into a frenzy of hostility whenever they see a white England football shirt on their TV screens, and vote for the equally staunch unionist Labour Party.

One of the most powerful arguments in favour of Scottish independence is precisely that it would remove a central cause of anti-English prejudice. Scotland's psyche has been forged by its status as a dependent nation, forced to submit politically to the will of its larger neighbour.

In the 1980s and early 1990s, when the Tories won four successive general elections in Britain, national tension in Scotland began to boil. In a confused way, anti-English sentiment became mixed together with anti-Toryism and working-class resentment against wealth and privilege. This was especially the case in some scenic rural areas, as affluent incomers from the booming South of England bought over property, driving up property prices and forcing locals in some instances to live in makeshift huts and caravans.

New Labour hoped the establishment of a Scottish Parliament would reduce these tensions. But, because the parliament has no powers over welfare, or employment, or nuclear weapons, and has only limited fiscal powers, that sense of political impotence will continue to fester. Especially if, at some stage in the future the Tory Party returned to government at Westminster, the embittered backlash in Scotland could make even the resentment of the Thatcher years appear like a lovers' tiff by comparison.

On the other hand, an independent Scotland with full control over its own economy, welfare system, and environment could eventually pave the way for the demise of anglophobia. In the early part of the 20th century, similar national tensions between the peoples of Norway and Sweden began to ease after Norway broke free, following a successful independence referendum. There has since evolved close co-operation among the Scandinavian countries; for example, the labour movements of the various countries campaign for common standards of welfare, wages, and conditions. There is also Scandinavia-wide co-ordination of railway timetables, roads, telecommunications, airlines, and postal services, even though the individual states remain politically independent of one another.

An independent Scotland would be forced to take responsibility for its own actions and could begin to forge a co-operative relationship with England on a free and equal basis rather than a subordinate relationship based on coercion and resentment.

Socialists should be prepared to support such a step, even on a non-socialist basis as promoted by the SNP. At the very least, the creation of an independent Scotland would begin to dispel the illusion that Scotland's problems could be solved simply by swapping the Union Flag for the St Andrew's Flag and replacing a right wing pro-market British government with a right-wing pro-market Scottish government. Democratic socialism, stronger today in Scotland than in any other part of the UK, would then be poised to become the main opposition force, and eventually the dominant force within an independent Scotland.

That doesn't mean winding up socialism in the meantime to concentrate on the fight for independence. That would only marginalize socialism and strengthen the hand of those right-wing nationalists who want to turn Scotland into a corporate colony with cheap labour, few public services, low business taxes, and oceans of profit for the transnationals. The strength of socialism in a future independent Scotland will be determined not just by what happens after the break-up of Britain, but by how effectively the ideas of socialism have permeated Scotland in the years leading up to independence.

There is no truth in the accusation that socialists who support the dissolution of the United Kingdom are anti-English, or anti-England. There is a difference between being anti-England and anti-United Kingdom. It is not England that oppresses Scotland and stifles its political development; it is the British state, which is controlled by a ruling class drawn from all four parts of the United Kingdom. But because England has seven times the population of the other three parts of the UK combined, its politics, economics, and culture have tended to dominate and submerge the rest. At the same time, national identity in all four parts of the UK has become warped and distorted – in England by a sense of superiority deriving from its dominant role in an imperialist state; in Scotland by a permanent sense of resentment towards its domineering neighbour.

For many people in Scotland, and in England too for that matter, English national identity can appear insular and backward-looking. When John Major outlined his view of English identity, he painted a romanticised picture of an Anglo-Saxon Brigadoon, complete with old maids cycling through autumn mists and rustic men sipping warm beer while watching cricket on the village green. A more sinister interpretation of English national identity is conveyed by tabloid newspapers like the English *Sun*, with their vile editorials abusing 'Krauts', 'Frogs', and 'Argies', and by the neo-Nazi cults and the football hooligans who spew imperial-racist mumbo-jumbo that would insult the intelligence of the average ten-year-old while brandishing the Flag of St George.

Socialists, naturally, oppose all forms of national chauvinism. It is right that socialists in England and Scotland stress their internationalist identity as part of the global working class. But on both sides of the border, socialists should also battle to rescue the progressive and inclusive sides of English and Scottish national identity.

In the 1950s, the American socialist leader James Cannon expressed regret that radicals in the United States had renounced the Fourth of July celebrations. 'It is wrong to confuse internationalism with anti-Americanism,' he argued.[7] Socialists in England, as well as in Scotland and Wales, should battle to reclaim the best of their national traditions from the jingoists and racists.

England is the land of great literary figures, such as Shakespeare, Shelley, Keats, Milton, Chaucer, Dickens, and many others. More recently, especially in the 1960s, it became the birthplace of some of the world's greatest and most innovative popular music. England also has an important radical and egalitarian tradition, running like a red thread through three centuries. English schoolchildren have traditionally been force-fed tales of the imperial adventures of successive monarchs, while the country's radical, democratic, and revolutionary tradition has been suppressed. This stretches back to the Levellers and the Diggers, the egalitarian revolutionary groups of the 17th century, and proceeds through to the Chartists, the militant struggles to establish the first industrial trade unions, the 1926 General Strike, and the three dramatic clashes between the National Union of Mineworkers and the Tories in the 1970s and 1980s.

Today, England is one of the most multicultural countries in Europe, with over 150 languages spoken on the streets of London alone. Indeed, neither England nor Scotland conforms to the racially pure myth peddled by fascist groups in Britain and by the white-supremacist descendants of Scottish settlers in the southern states of the USA.

Like England, Scotland has changed down through the ages, culturally, linguistically, and socially. The entire history of the country has been one of emigration and immigration. From Ireland, Scandinavia, England, Northern Europe, Eastern Europe, Italy, Pakistan, India, and China, successive waves of settlers have poured into Scotland over the centuries.

As the novelist William McIlvanney once memorably put it, 'The Scots are a mongrel race.' In Scotland today we have Asian-born Scots, Irish-born Scots, English-born Scots, Italian-born Scots, and Scottish-born Scots. We have Gaelic-speaking Scots, Doric-speaking Scots, and English-speaking Scots. We have Highland Scots, Lowland Scots, and Scots in the Northern Isles whose historic links are with Scandinavia.

A socialist Scotland would aim to break down prejudices and rivalries within Scotland, while allowing a large degree of autonomy for any community – geographical, ethnic, or linguistic – which sought a measure of control over its own affairs. It would fight for the survival of the Gaelic language and ensure that everyone who wants to learn the ancient tongue has the opportunity to do so. In the past, Scotland's native cultural traditions were brutally suppressed in the past by London governments and their Scottish unionist allies. Today, the threat to Scots or Gaelic culture tends to come from media moguls such as Rupert Murdoch, whose worldwide ownership of newspapers and TV and radio stations enables them to exert a poisonous influence over the development of culture in all countries, large and small.

But an independent socialist Scotland would not be an isolationist Scotland. It would not involve rebuilding Hadrian's Wall and quarantining ourselves from the rest of the world. Instead, a socialist Scotland would be forward-looking and outward-looking. It would immediately build links with political, environmental, trade-union, and pro-democracy movements all over the globe to launch a united worldwide crusade against global capitalism.

The other side of globalisation is that even the slightest crack in the structure would weaken the entire edifice. The system may today seem invincible. At the start of the 1980s, Stalinism seemed like an indestructible monolith. In the mid-1980s, the apartheid regime in South Africa looked impregnable. The whole history of the 20th century illustrates that institutions, governments, and social systems which one day appear to be as permanent as the sun and the moon can the next day become history.

Any serious move towards democratic socialism in the 21st century, in Scotland or in any other country, would have earth-shattering consequences. At the very least, a successful challenge to capitalism in Scotland would attract worldwide sympathy and would help to dramatically accelerate the advance of genuine democratic socialism internationally.

Chapter Eighteen

THE TARTAN REVOLUTION

ONE OF THE most impressive buildings in Scotland stands towering over Edinburgh's Princes Street. It's not quite so imposing as Edinburgh Castle, a hundred yards to the west. But this vast four-storey edifice, with its ornate windows, its hand-carved statues, its intricate domes and turrets, stands as a monumental symbol to the power of money.

The building is the headquarters of one of Scotland's wealthiest institutions, the Bank of Scotland. In the financial year up to April 2000, the Bank made over £1 billion in profit. So too did its arch-rival on the other side of Princes Street, the Royal Bank of Scotland. The profits of these two institutions alone are more than enough to provide an extra £45 a week for every pensioner in Scotland; or to increase spending on the NHS by 50 per cent; or to construct a brand-new state-of-the-art metro system in Greater Glasgow or in the Lothians; or to demolish 25,000 substandard homes and replace them with brand-new back-and-front-door houses with gardens.

Scotland is a fabulously wealthy country. This is not the impoverished Nicaragua of the 1980s, which was brought to its knees by an American economic blockade. Measured by the total amount of goods and services produced per head, Scotland is today ten times richer than Russia, which was once the world's second superpower. It is 15 times richer than Cuba and probably 100 times wealthier than Cuba at the time of the revolution led by Fidel Castro and Che Guevara in 1959.[1]

We are told by all the main political parties that global capitalism is too powerful to be resisted. Scotland is too small, too weak, too poor, to make a stand. All we can do is plead for more resources from Westminster while rattling the begging bowl in front of the transnational corporations in the hope that they will invest a few crumbs more.

There is, however, an alternative road forward. We could begin the fight now for an independent democratic socialist Scotland, which will stand up to the forces of global capitalism and become an international symbol of resistance to economic and social injustice.

The material foundations already exist in Scotland for a thriving, blossoming socialist democracy which would be an inspiration to the working class, the young, the poor and the dispossessed the world over. We have land, water, fish, timber, oil, gas and electricity in abundance. We have a moderate climate, where floods, droughts, and hurricanes are almost unknown. The winds that howl in from the Atlantic have phenomenal potential to provide a new source of permanent energy which does not pollute the planet. While other countries face problems of congestion and overcrowding, we have vast wildernesses that are today virtually uninhabited. We have a clean environment and tens of thousands of miles of coastline that can be utilised for trade, fishing and tourism.

We have a highly skilled workforce and an educated population. Only two other countries in the world have more accredited academic papers published per head of population. More than a quarter of Scotland's total workforce has top-level academic or managerial qualifications. We have a long tradition of science and engineering. The cultural side of Scottish life is flourishing as never before with legions of internationally acclaimed musicians, writers, actors, and film directors.

Yet Scotland today is scarred by poverty, low pay, sub-standard housing, crime, alcohol abuse, heroin addiction and ill health. It is a tragic indictment of the social system we live under that, in the 21st century, people living in the poorest areas of Scotland can expect to die eight years younger than those living in the most prosperous areas.[2]

This glaring contradiction between the potential and the reality has one simple explanation: the people of Scotland have no real control over our wealth and resources. Our land is owned by upper-class lairds and absentee landlords. Our oil, gas and electricity is owned by business tycoons. Our financial institutions are controlled by multimillionaire bankers. Even our schools and hospitals are being turned over to the private profiteers.

A fully-fledged socialist society could never be achieved within the borders of a small country such as Scotland. The eradication of all social and economic inequality could only be achieved on an all-European, or perhaps even a world scale. Nonetheless, a Scottish socialist government could at least begin to move in the direction of socialism by taking control over key sectors of the economy, by introducing workplace and community democracy, and by implementing radical and popular reforms which would set an example for other countries to follow.

A new socialist economy would be based on a range of different types of enterprises with the emphasis on social ownership. Large-scale industry, oil, gas, electricity, the national railway network could be owned by the people of Scotland as a whole and run by democratically elected boards in which workers, consumers, and the wider socialist government were all repre-sented. These would not be based on the old-style nationalisation projects. Instead of centralised planning by a remote bureaucracy, there could be decentralised democratic planning using the most advanced information technology. Where practically possible, socially owned enterprises could be broken down into smaller sub-units to enable closer scrutiny by the wider public.

Social ownership could also involve community-owned and municipally-owned companies. Municipally-owned building companies could be established to build new homes, schools, community centres, sports centres and other local facilities. Local bus and underground systems too could be taken over and run by the larger councils, or jointly by neighbouring smaller councils.

Another form of social ownership that could be encouraged through the provision of cheap loans and other incentives would be workers' co-operatives. Repeated studies have shown that when employees own and run their own companies, they work harder and more efficiently. Following one of the most in-depth studies ever carried out, based on research in the UK, Greece, Italy, Spain, Cyprus, and Malta, one expert, Dr Godfrey Baldacchino of the University of Malta concluded, 'Worker-owners typically work better, they work harder, they offer competitive services, they distribute their gains more equitably, they enjoy high levels of participation in decision-making and they enjoy high levels of job satisfaction.'[3]

In a socialist Scotland, some sections of the economy would most likely remain in private hands. It would be absurd for any socialist government to try to take over small shops, ice cream vans, Indian takeaways, taxi-cab firms, car mechanics yards and the multitude of other small-scale enterprises which play a central role in producing goods and delivering services.

In total, there are just under 300,000 businesses in Scotland. Only 1.2 per cent of these employ over 50 people, while at the other end of the spectrum, 93.7 per cent of businesses employ less than ten people. In a socialist Scotland, these hundreds of thousands of small businesses would thrive because they would be competing with each other on a level playing field, rather than competing with big business on similar terms that the Christians competed with the lions in ancient Rome.

Some larger companies, too, may even remain in private hands on the grounds of expediency. For example, there are now almost 40,000 workers employed in Scottish call centres, most of which have been set up by outside companies based in England or abroad. Attempting to take a call centre into public ownership is likely to be a futile gesture: it would literally stop functioning overnight, leaving banks of silent telephones. Similarly, some branch assembly plants, particularly in the electronics sector, are individual links in an international production chain.

In these instances, a socialist government could enforce certain basic standards of wages and conditions, including a minimum wage of at least a £7 an hour (at today's values); trade-union rights; a shorter working week; and workers' control over health, safety, and other workplace conditions.

Companies which refused to meet these conditions would forfeit their assets. They could also be forced by law to provide minimum redundancy payments, perhaps the equivalent of two to three years' wages, to allow a reasonable time for the sacked workers to be retrained and redeployed.

Today in Scotland, each worker employed by a foreign-owned company produces on average an astonishing £184,000 of wealth. By contrast, capital investment in these companies adds up to just £7600 per employee. Even with vastly increased wages, improved conditions, shorter hours, and higher rates of corporation tax, most companies would probably still find it profitable to remain.[4]

But, within a socialist Scotland, the private sector would be subordinate to the social sector. Profit would no longer be the *raison d'etre* of all economic activity. Instead of being siphoned off to shareholders, the surpluses produced by workers would be used to increase wages, reduce hours, improve working conditions, develop public services, and boost investment. Social and environmental considerations would take precedence, as would longer-term planning and training.

If the minutes of the board meetings of, for example, Scotland's giant construction companies were publicly available – which they're not – they would no doubt be preoccupied with questions such as: 'How can we cut costs? Where can we make redundancies? Where will we advertise? Where can we get cheaper materials? Is there any land up for sale that is likely to increase in value? How much can we increase the cost of a new three-bedroom house without losing market share? Can we work out a strategy for driving some of our rivals out of business?'

Within a socialist economy, the elected board of a socially owned construction firm could have a different agenda. It could discuss such questions as: 'What are the latest homelessness figures and how are we tackling the problem? What are the results of the tenants' consultation over the design options for the new council estate in the East End of Glasgow? Are the materials we are using on this project sufficiently durable? Will the houses be properly insulated to save energy? Will they be barrier-free to make them suitable for disabled residents? Can we reduce the price of a new three-bedroom home? Are safety standards on our sites being adhered to? Are we in a position yet to move from a four-day week to a three-and-a-half-day week?'

There could be total transparency in the workings of all branches of the economy, with minutes of every board meeting of all large enterprises published online. There would be mechanisms to ensure that board members could be removed from their positions at any time by those who elected them. Although there would be the need for managerial and technical specialists, whose salaries would be subject to negotiation, board members themselves would receive no more than the average wage of a skilled worker in that industry.

To survive and thrive, any economy must constantly innovate. Yet the total amount spent on research and development in Scotland in 1999 was just £330 million, less than two per cent of the £18 billion profit bonanza made in Scotland in the same year by just 20 companies.[5] Scotland has the skills and technology to develop its own socially owned electronics, information technology, and chemical industries which would not be at the mercy of boards of directors in distant cities.

There are hundreds of thousands of websites devoted to radical environmentalism, anti-capitalism, and socialism. A socialist Scotland could utilise communications technology, not only to generate international political solidarity, but also to open up trade with this potentially massive radical cybermarket.

Such far-reaching change could not be carried through without full political and economic independence. The devolved semi-parliament at Holyrood, with its lack of economic muscle, could not even begin to scratch the surface of inequality in Scotland. Nor could the SNP's alternative to devolution – Independence in Europe within a single European currency – offer genuine independence. Control over economic policy would simply shift from Westminster and the Bank of England to Brussels and the European Central Bank. And, like their London-based counterparts, the bankers, bureaucrats, and big-business-oriented politicians who run the European Union will fiercely resist any serious attempt to build a more egalitarian society in Scotland, or in any other European country.

A socialist government in Scotland would require to create its own central bank. It would bring the other major banks and financial institutions into the public sector and establish a network of community banks, building societies, and insurance companies. Based on the same principles on which credit unions operate in many local communities, a new socialist financial system could provide low-interest credit, attractive savings terms, and cheap insurance. It would especially benefit farmers, small businesses, and workers' co-operatives.

For most mainstream politicians, the idea of banks being owned by the people rather than by private shareholders is unthinkable. Banks, after all, are the private property of rich individuals to run as they see fit. You can't just deprive these people of their livelihood as though they were shipyard workers, or miners, or machine operators.

In a socialist Scotland, this culture of deference to the rich and powerful will be dissolved. Just as capitalism set out to abolish 'the divine right of kings', socialism will set out to abolish the divine right of bankers, shareholders, and stockbrokers. The needs of society as a whole will eventually be elevated above convention, tradition, and sentiment.

Certainly, shareholders would be compensated. A democratically elected compensation board could be established, which was representative of society as a whole. It would try to arrive at a fair settlement with shareholders to ensure that they were not driven into debt, bankruptcy, and poverty. But there would be no question of doling out millions of pounds in compensation to wealthy individuals, as previous Labour government did when they nationalised industries such as coal, rail, and steel.

Publicly owned banks exist even in the most right-wing free-market societies. In the United States, the Federal Reserve is state-owned. The European Central Bank, too, is owned not by private shareholders but by the member states of the European Union. The Bank of France and the Bank of England are publicly owned. Even Russia under Boris Yeltsin, after privatising three quarters of all public enterprises was forced to nationalise some of the country's biggest banks when the Moscow stock exchange went into free fall in the late 1990s.

There are thousands of examples of local, regional, and national banks and financial institutions that are socially owned in one form or another. Most building societies and many insurance companies – including one of Scotland's biggest financial institutions, Standard Life – were built, not as profit-making businesses but as mutuals, owned by their customers. In a significant rejection of the smash-and-grab culture of free-market capitalism, Standard Life's two million policy-holders recently voted to retain the company's mutual status, rejecting bribes worth an average of £6000 per person to float it on the stock exchange.

Neither Standard Life nor any of these other institutions are run democratically. None are run remotely in the interests of the wider community. All of them are subservient to the demands of private capital. Nonetheless, the fact that publicly owned banks and mutual insurance companies exist and thrive even in the heartlands of free-market capitalism is an answer to those who argue that public ownership of finance is impractical.

Some politicians, even on the Left of the political spectrum, express fear that radical measures directed against the banks and other capitalist institutions would provoke a 'flight of capital'. Naturally, a socialist government would try to counter that with immediate legislation restricting the amount of money that could be shifted out of the country. Before Thatcher rewrote the rules in the early 1980s, even the British government, along every other government in the world, had strict controls on the movement of capital in and out of the country.

In today's hi-tech economy, it is much easier to shift capital around. But a financial system is more than just money. It consists of physical resources: staff, buildings, computers, cash machines. It is built upon expertise. Whether any financial system can function effectively or not depends first and foremost on the skills, the training, the know-how, the experience of the workforce at every level.

Money can be shuffled around from one country to another. But an entire financial system employing 100,000 skilled and trained workers cannot just be dismantled and moved abroad.

In any case, most of the operations of the financial sharks who shift money around are purely parasitical. They are like touts buying up tickets for a big cup final so that they can later sell them at five times their original value. They create nothing and add nothing to the general welfare of society. As things stand today, only a small fraction of the £300 billion controlled by Edinburgh's financial institutions is actually invested in the Scottish economy.

One argument against socialism that has been checkmated by the development of information technology is the claim that democratic planning is impossible in a complex society. 'Let the market decide!' is the cry of the profiteers. They rightly denounce the centralised bureaucratic planning of the economy that contributed to the downfall of the Soviet Union.

But the creation of a democratically co-ordinated, harmonious, integrated economy is more viable today than ever before. Information technology can track sales, prices, distribution, and a mass of other relevant data. It can make instantaneous adjustments where necessary. Even now, the big supermarkets operate a system whereby every sale is recorded in a centralised database, which in turn is linked to a series of warehouses. Computerised order books then instantaneously calculate which stocks need to be replenished.

In other words, production is planned. But, under capitalism, such commercial planning is limited and fragmented. It is also highly secretive. Information is jealously hoarded by each individual company and exploited for commercial gain. If an item is selling well, the price will be jacked up to the highest level the market will tolerate. The prices of other goods will be temporarily slashed as a means of undercutting competitors and eventually driving them out of business.

Under capitalism, the flow of information that has been made possible by computer technology is abused for private profit. Under a socialist economy, these information systems would be expanded and integrated across the economy, and they would be geared to the broad needs of society as a whole, rather than to the narrow demands of company shareholders.

It would be foolhardy at this stage to even attempt to set out an *exact* blueprint of how a socially owned economy in Scotland would function in fine detail. There would be continual improvisation and fine-tuning on the basis of experience.

Moreover, the establishment of an independent socialist Scotland would only be a transitional step towards a wider international socialist confederation. It is an open question whether the battle for socialism across Europe will be pioneered in Scotland or whether the people in Scotland will follow a trail first blazed elsewhere.

There is no arguing with the fact that capitalism ended the 20th century triumphant. But, as the 21st century progresses and the mists of confusion begin to be dispelled, the idea of socialism will emerge more clearly and powerfully than ever before. Socialism's time may not yet have come, but 'it's comin' yet for a' that'.

Chapter Nineteen

LESS EQUAL THAN OTHERS

PRINCES STREET GARDENS is one of the more colourful parts of Edinburgh city centre. When the summer sun beats down on the lush green lawns, it's hard to imagine that this urban oasis was once submerged under the notorious Nor' Loch.

Back in the Middle Ages, women suspected of practising witchcraft would be thrown into the Nor' Loch to establish whether or not they were guilty. If the wretched victim drowned, this meant she could be pronounced innocent. If she failed to drown, this was proof that she was indeed a witch, so she was burned at the stake.

Today, we shudder with horror at stories of medieval superstition and prejudice. Thankfully, we live in the enlightened 21st century, where bigotry and intolerance no longer exist. Unless you happen to be black or Asian, that is. Or unless you happen to be gay. Or you're a Muslim, a Sikh, a Hindu, or a Jew. Or a Catholic in some parts of Scotland or a Protestant in others. Or you speak with an English accent. Or you're a single parent. Or you're in some way different from everyone else.

During the Euro 2000 tournament, England football fans were filmed brandishing Union Jacks and Flags of St George and chanting the most infantile racist claptrap. Oblivious to the irony, these swaggering bigots sang hymns of praise celebrating the 'English victory' in the Second World War, while spewing out notions of racial superiority which would have gladdened the heart of Adolf Hitler himself.

It would be foolish to pretend that Scotland is somehow morally superior to England or to anywhere else. There are parts of this country where the Asian community lives under a permanent reign of terror. Gay people are frequently targeted, not just for verbal abuse, but for violent physical attack and even murder. On the Saturday night of a Celtic-Rangers match, Glasgow city centre can sometimes resemble a war zone as alcohol-fuelled sectarian tribalism erupts into bloody violence.

On the other hand, there is no doubt that, overall, Scotland is gradually becoming a more tolerant society. In the inter-war years, the Borders-born writer, John Buchan, wrote of 'fat Jews', 'blue-black dagos', 'filthy Kaffirs' (ie black South Africans). His works are littered with derogatory references to races he clearly regarded as sub-human. Yet Buchan was exalted by the literary establishment, and was a respectable Tory politician, to boot.[1]

Nowadays, though some of the party's policies have subtle racist undertones, even respectable Tory politicians are not quite so blatantly racist. The only open racist party that operates in Scotland, the fascist British National Party, received less than half of one per cent of the vote in the 1999 European elections – less than one tenth of the support gained by parties committed to the socialist transformation of society.

Even sectarianism, for generations the scourge of Scotland, is in long-term retreat. In the cosmopolitan Edinburgh of the 21st century, it's hard to believe that a few generations ago, in 1936, a political party which stood for the expulsion of all Catholics from Scotland, took 31 per cent of the vote across the city. The party, Protestant Action, won a number of council seats and remained a major force in the capital throughout the 1930s. A similar vote was achieved by the Scottish Protestant League in Glasgow during the same period. More recently, at the end of the

1980s, Rangers supporters burned their scarves in protest at the signing of a Catholic footballer, Mo Johnston. Yet within a decade Rangers were regularly fielding more Catholics in their first team than their arch-rivals, Celtic – and the only bonfires in the West of Scotland these days take place on Guy Fawkes Night.

Anti-gay prejudice – homophobia – is also less pronounced than in the past, notwithstanding the hysterical crusade waged by tabloid newspapers and church leaders. In the postal referendum organised by the campaign to keep Section 28, fewer than one in four Scots voted to retain the legislation, despite the high-profile multi-million-pound campaign urging people to vote. In the only comparable referendum in recent times – the Strathclyde water referendum in 1994, which was also a postal ballot conducted along similar lines – three out of four people voted to keep water public.

Socialists welcome this changing culture for two reasons. Firstly, because genuine socialism is about encouraging tolerance and diversity and opposing coercion and repression. People who are gay, or black, or Jewish, or Muslim, or English, or Irish, have as much right to get on with their lives without harassment as people who have red hair, or people who wear baseball caps.

And secondly, because racism, bigotry, and sectarianism can only weaken the capacity of working people to organise themselves against exploitation and injustice. There have been many occasions in history when the rich and powerful have deliberately used such divisions to set ordinary people at each others' throats – black against white, Protestant against Catholic, Hindu against Muslim, Christian against Jew. At its most extreme, racism and xenophobia can result in the barbarous bloodletting that has turned much of the Balkans into a hell on earth over the past decade or so.

At this stage, Western European racism, personified by people like Haider in Austria and Le Pen in France, has attempted to cultivate a more respectable image. But, faced with serious economic and social crisis in the future, politics could turn ugly even in some of the most apparently civilised countries.

Many people who would not dream of discriminating against another human being on the grounds of race or religion will nonetheless cheerfully accept discrimination on the grounds of sex. After all, on the face of it, sexism does not have the same potential for violent division as racism or sectarianism. We've all read about race riots and holy wars, but relations between the sexes are so intimately intertwined as to preclude such extreme conflict.

Certainly, prejudice against women tends to be more insidious than the irrational hatred that is the standard hallmark of racism, sectarianism, and homophobia. But it can and does lead to violence. There are infinitely more violent assaults by men against women in Scotland than there are racist or sectarian attacks. Most of these assaults take place in the home and, in the most extreme cases, end in murder. And most violence against women stems from traditional superstitions of male superiority that still hold sway even in the 21st century. For many centuries – indeed right up until the end of the 19th century – men were even entitled by law to use physical violence in the home to impose their authority over women

Just as racism, sectarianism, and homophobia have tended to lessen over the years, attitudes towards women, too, have undergone profound changes over the generations. At the beginning of the 20th century, no woman anywhere in the world was entitled to vote. By the late 20th century, a majority of women had won the right to vote, while a minority, including Margaret Thatcher, Benazir Bhutto, Indira Gandhi and Golda Meir, were even able to rise to positions of immense political power.

In the more advanced countries, women have achieved legal rights to equal pay, divorce, contraception, and abortion. Although housework still consumes vast amounts of time and energy, especially for women with young children, the development of household appliances, such as washing machines, cookers, fridge-freezers, vacuum cleaners, and microwave ovens, has relieved at least some of the drudgery that had been their lot. And increasingly, women have been drawn into the workplace – to the point where they now constitute the majority of the workforce in Britain.

These changes have led some women from more privileged backgrounds to draw the conclusion that equality between the sexes has already been achieved. Some of the most vocal feminists of the past now describe themselves as 'post-feminists'. But while a minority of women, especially those from the more privileged social classes, have been able to take advantage of the new climate, the vast majority of women across the world remain doubly oppressed, doubly exploited, under capitalism.

On a global scale, almost 70 per cent of all work is carried out by women. Yet they receive ten per cent of the world's income and own barely one per cent of the world's wealth. Women make up just over 50 per cent of the world's population; yet 70 per cent of people living in absolute poverty in the world today are women.[3]

Even in the most advanced liberal democracies, where formal legal equality has been enshrined in the statue books, women remain second-class citizens. In Scotland, even though girls tend to show more academic potential at school than boys, by the time they reach adulthood women are usually relegated to subordinate roles. Often, they work in the most low-paid soul-destroying occupations.

Three quarters of catering and basic-grade clerical workers are women. Women earn, on average, 20 per cent less than men. They shoulder most of the burden of child-rearing, housework, dealing with debt, and coping with domestic crises. Within local communities, it is invariably women who undertake the bulk of the unpaid voluntary work which makes life a little more bearable for children, for the elderly, and for others who would otherwise be socially excluded.

In the 19th century, the leader of the General German Workers' Association, Ferdinand Lassalle, claimed that 'The rightful work of women and mothers is in the home and family . . . women and mothers should absorb themselves in the cosiness and poetry of domestic life.'

If such attitudes were expressed today by a trade union or socialist leader, they would be treated with derision and contempt. In Britain today, 60 per cent of household breadwinners are women. Yet women still have a long hard road to travel before they arrive at social and economic liberation.

A lifestyle survey conducted in June 2000 by *Top Santé* magazine blew away the media myth of the 21st-century 'superwoman' who effortlessly juggles motherhood, family life, and a successful career with motherhood and family life. Of the 5000 women surveyed, 75 per cent considered themselves underpaid for the work that they do, 70 per cent said they were overworked; and 77 per cent believed that work-related stress was damaging their health. Overall, no fewer than 79 per cent of women said they were disillusioned with the world of work.

The survey showed that, in Scotland, 90 per cent of women do most of the household chores and shoulder most of the responsibility for the children, even where both partners are working full time. Instead of gaining social liberation, working women with children are gaining the worst of all worlds. They are forced to work full time in dead-end underpaid jobs to help pay household bills. They then return to face a second full-time job in the home. Life can become an endless treadmill of mind-numbing drudgery, mental stress, and physical exhaustion. And although today's generation of women are more confident, more independent, and more free to make their own choices, they still endure many of the pressures that their mothers and grandmothers had to face.

Some women, naturally and understandably, blame men for women's oppression. They believe women would be liberated if only men would change their attitudes. But the problem of sexual inequality runs much deeper. It is rooted in the basic structures of the society we live in.

The traditional family, as portrayed in TV adverts, is often held up as the only natural way for people to live. Yet the family, as we know it today, is a relatively recent institution. And like every other institution in society, the family unit has evolved and developed over many centuries, in line with economic changes.

In his pioneering work, *Origins of the Family, Private Property and the State* first published in 1886, Friedrich Engels traced the development of human relations from the earliest primitive societies. Some of the detail of the book could be corrected in the light of 20th-century anthropological discoveries. Nonetheless, Engels' basic analysis of the evolution of the family has stood the test of time and scrutiny.[4]

He described how ancient tribal societies were characterised by social equality. Land was held in common and resources were shared out in a form of elementary socialism. In this type of society, relations between the sexes were much less rigid because there was no wealth to pass on to future generations – and therefore paternity was not considered all that important.

In his book, *Highlanders: A History of the Gaels*, the writer John MacLeod, ironically a partisan of the fundamentalist Free Presbyterian Church, provides precise corroboration of Engels' description of ancient society. Although he seems slightly bemused at his discovery, MacLeod provides the following honest description of life in the early Highland clans:

'Even more oddly, they had no institution of marriage. Men and women lived in what we would today call free love, and children were raised by the whole clan and not as part of a smaller family unit. As paternity would have been a matter of great argument — had they greatly cared — succession to all offices came through the female line.'

Although he fails to make the connection between the absence of private family structures and the absence of personal property, MacLeod goes on to explain that, in the Highlands at that time, 'Land belonged to no individual but to the whole clan.'[5]

Later, when men began to personally acquire land, livestock, and slaves, they also began to wonder what would happen to their possessions after they died. The idea of the private family began to take root. Women became the property of their husbands, as did the children of the marriage. Then, after the death of the husband, land and other possessions were handed down through the generations.

In other words, the institution of marriage, rather than representing the highest expression of romantic love in the best Mills and Boon tradition, actually evolved as a business arrangement. Before that business arrangement was established, women were strong and equal to men. Afterwards, they became the private property of their husbands and the roots of discrimination and oppression were planted.

Many people choose to live in what are usually described as 'traditional' families. Many of these families are based on mutual love and support on a free and equal basis. For a lot of people — women, men, and children — family life can offer an oasis of affection, warmth, and security in a harsh and hostile world. But, for others, the traditional family can be a prison from which there is little prospect of escape. A quarter of all violent attacks take place in the home; most female murder victims die at the hands of their male partners; many others suffer psychological torture within the marital home, yet, because of economic and social pressures find it almost impossible to leave.[6]

Today, some politicians and church leaders campaign for a return to 'traditional family values' and insist on elevating the virtues of this type of family, sanctified by the marriage ceremony, above all other living arrangements. Backed by sections of the tabloid press, they denounce one-parent families, people who are gay or lesbian, and everyone else whose lifestyle doesn't fit the conventional pattern. Yet many non-traditional families do provide love, compassion, and security for children.

Democratic socialism is an extremely tolerant philosophy. But one thing that a future socialist Scotland will not tolerate is intolerance. In 18th-century Scotland, ministers would implore church congregations to report any sins against the sexual moral code of Calvinism. Sinners thus exposed were forced to sit in a special seat in the Kirk called the 'Creepie Chair', where they were mercilessly denounced before the entire congregation. With the full force of his eloquent invective, Robert Burns scornfully lampooned this hypocrisy in poems such as *Address to the Unco Guid*:

> 'Oh ye, wha are sae guid yersel'
> Sae pious and sae holy,
> Wi' nowt to do but mark and tell
> Your neebours' faults and folly!'

Today, the role of society's moral Gestapo has largely been taken over by the tabloid press. Private lives are paraded across the front pages, the modern equivalent of the 'Creepie Chair'. One-parent families, people who are gay or lesbian, and others who don't conform to tradition and convention are treated as the enemies within, a subversive mob undermining the foundations of society.

But blaming one-parent families for undermining traditional values is like blaming reservoirs for the rain. It is to confuse cause and effect. Over the past 30 years, the number of one-parent families in Britain has multiplied six-fold; however, this is a symptom of the failure of the traditional structures of society, rather than the cause of that failure.

As a general rule, lone parents don't choose to become lone parents. Contrary to the impression created by some journalists and politicians, most lone parents are not irresponsible teenagers who have deliberately become pregnant to scrounge welfare benefits and jump the housing queue. In fact, fewer than one in 20 are in their teens. Two out of three are separated, divorced, or widowed. And most live on the breadline. While seven per cent of married couples have a total income amounting to less than £150 a week, 59 per cent of lone parents are in this category. Whatever anyone may claim, single parenthood is no bed of roses.[7]

Yet, like Humpty Dumpty, traditional family values cannot be put back together again, either by introducing legislation or by waging moral crusades. The stresses and strains that bear down on women and men, distort their relationships, and damage the psychological and physical welfare of children, will not be relieved by trying to turn the omelette back into an egg.

A socialist Scotland would aim to shift major resources towards ensuring the welfare of children and towards relieving the drudgery and pressure that many women face. Instead of people being left to tackle these problems privately, they could be tackled socially.

Child care, for example, is a huge predicament for most women and families with young children With the decline of extended families, in which grandparents, aunts, and uncles would all tend to live in close proximity, women with young children can no longer rely on the broad network of support which their parents, and especially their grandparents, could count upon.

Within a socialist Scotland, a network of community crèches and round-the-clock child-care centres could be established. All workplaces over a certain size could be compelled to provide nursery facilities. The introduction of a shorter working week with flexible hours, and longer holidays synchronised with school holidays would allow women and men to spend more time with their children. By extending paid maternity and paternity leave to a period of several years – to be taken in any combination – parents could be freed to spend time with their young children without giving up their jobs or undermining their promotion prospects.

Within a socialist system, a radical new benefits system could be introduced that recognised the crucial social role that women in particular play. A parent who wanted to give up work to look after children full time, even to educate children at home, could be given that option.

Full-time carers – again mainly women – are scandalously exploited by society. They dedicate their lives to looking after people who are too old, too ill, or too infirm to look after themselves. Without their devotion and selflessness, our social services and health service would be at breaking point. Yet the average allowance paid to a full-time carer is just £40 a week. A socialist welfare system could guarantee at least the equivalent of the national minimum wage to all those who devote themselves full time to looking after children, elderly people, or disabled people.

In addition, social-support systems could be developed to break down the isolation of those confined to home full time, either because they are carers or because they are being cared for. This could include community-based adult education and training; breakfast, lunch, and dinner clubs; sporting and cultural activities; and safe, supervised play areas for children in every locality.

In a future socialist Scotland, even the time-consuming grind of domestic housework could be partly relieved by social initiatives. For example, high quality eat-in and take-away restaurants, offering good food at low prices, could be established in every neighbourhood. Door-to-door laundry, ironing, and even house cleaning, could be organised at community level for those who wanted to use such a service. Many affluent households today employ housekeepers, often at pitifully low rates of pay. By contrast, workers employed in community household services in a socialist Scotland would receive trade-union rates of pay and union-negotiated hours and conditions.

A 50–50 division of household labour between the sexes could also be encouraged by a socialist government. That is not to suggest that harmonious relationships can ever be imposed through legislation; but by providing the necessary social infrastructure, backed by serious financial resources, we could at least lay the foundations for a society based on genuine equality between the sexes.

A socially oriented society would be geared especially towards those who are most powerless in the privatised society we live in today. Young children, elderly people, those who suffer from severe disabilities, would no longer be treated as though they were some kind of burden, but would become valued members of society with an important contribution to make.

Not just human beings, but animals too, could be freed from needless physical and psychological suffering. Hunting with hounds, intensive factory farming, the export and import of live animals, cosmetic testing, and other forms of cruelty against animals would have no place in a future socialist Scotland.

It would be absurd to claim that economic and social changes alone can create a society of genuine equality, free from racism, sectarianism, prejudice, bigotry, and discrimination. These stains will take generations to wash away without trace. But, in the meantime, we can at least begin to move towards a society in which ideals such as solidarity, respect, and co-operation are elevated above values such as greed, cynicism, and ruthlessness.

Chapter Twenty

PAINTING A BRIGHTER FUTURE

SOME PEOPLE HATE capitalism and its values, yet remain uneasy about socialism. One of their strongest misgivings is that a socialist society would be drab. They fear that a society based on social equality would be a monotonous, conformist society in which individualism is frowned upon and that there would be no room for talent or diversity.

People are, after all, unique. There are six billion human beings on the planet, yet so complex is our genetic make-up that each one of these six billion people has a different personality from everyone else. There may be national characteristics forged by historical, geographical, and economic circumstances. Communities may have developed their own shared value systems. But within these nations and communities, everyone has their own characteristics, their own special aptitudes and talents, their own particular combination of virtues and vices, their own inimitable use of language, their own idiosyncratic gestures and facial expressions. If you unexpectedly met one of your neighbours in a crowded street in a far-off city, you would recognise them immediately, so distinctive are individual human beings even in their superficial appearance.

Anyone who fears that socialism is about sameness, or that social equality is about uniformity, is one thousand per cent mistaken. They have spectacularly misunderstood what socialism is all about. Socialism is not about regimentation; it is about building a society where diversity, originality, individuality, creativity, and ingenuity will be allowed to truly flourish for the first time in human history.

One of the most extraordinary myths that has gained widespread acceptance across society, even on the part of people who should know better, is that capitalism encourages freedom and diversity. That was partially true in the early days of capitalism, when the rising merchant classes were forced to wage war against the kings and queens and lords and archbishops in order to break down the rigid authoritarian structures of feudalism.

Shakespeare's *Romeo and Juliet*, for example – which seems a harmless enough little romance to us today – was regarded back in the 16th century as a subversive piece of drama, because it promoted the ideal of a society where young people should be free to choose their own partners on the basis of mutual attraction.

In its day, the idea of free romantic love was as controversial as the recent row over Section 28 in Scotland; in the Middle Ages, the social norm was compulsory arranged marriage. *Romeo and Juliet* was written on behalf of the rising new merchant classes, who were striving to remove the petty restrictions of feudalism and create a society in which they would be free to pursue commerce and make themselves rich.

But capitalism in the 21st century has become as big an obstacle blocking the path of human development as feudalism in the 16th and 17th centuries. Ironically, this system which generates astonishing economic and social inequalities simultaneously breeds grey uniformity in all aspects of human art and culture. And, in an added twist, as capitalism develops economically, human society and culture becomes ever more standardised and monotonous

Travel to any city anywhere in the world and you'll see the same fast-food restaurants – the McDonalds, the Burger Kings, the Kentucky Fried Chickens – selling the same bland food. The more modern the city is, the more tedious the architecture. People wear the same clothes with the same designer labels. Go into a bar – and the chances are there'll be shillelaghs and Gaelic road signs hanging from the walls – and buy the same beer and listen to the same music on the jukebox. Go into the cinema and you'll see the same Hollywood blockbusters, perhaps dubbed or subtitled into the appropriate local language. Turn on the TV and you'll see *Frasier* and *Friends* and local variations of British soap operas and quiz shows.

Increasingly, we are living in a monocultural society driven by the power of money and subservient to the rule of profit. Have you ever wondered why Santa Claus wears a red coat with white trimmings? Perhaps it derives from some ancient tradition or denotes some special religious significance from centuries long past? Wrong. Santa wears red and white because these are the corporate colours of Coca-Cola. What we have been all too easily deluded into imagining is a traditional icon was actually devised as an advertising stunt in 1931 by Coca-Cola, who dressed up Father Christmas in the company's distinctive colour scheme.

That was 70 years ago – and the power of corporate capitalism is a million times stronger today. More and more, it dictates which films we see, which TV programmes we watch, which music we listen to, which football team we support, which T-shirt we wear, which foods we eat, which beers we drink, which books we read. Fortunately, there are plenty of courageous writers, poets, publishers, musicians, film-makers, painters, sculptors, who refuse to sell their talent to the highest bidder.

In the past, Scotland used to churn out a disproportionately large number of world-class footballers for such a small nation. Sadly, those days seem to have vanished. But who would have imagined back then that Scotland would eventually emerge as a major force in the world of literature and film? With writers and poets such as James Kelman, Alasdair Gray, William McIlvanney, Iain Banks, Janice Galloway, Irvine Welsh,

Alan Spence, Alison Kennedy, Alan Warner, Ian McEwan, Laura Hird, John Burnside, Tom Leonard, Edwin Morgan, Toni Davidson, Carol Ann Duffy, Robert Crawford, Duncan McLean, Don Paterson, Jeff Torrington, Jackie Kay, Michel Faber, Gordon Legge, Angus Calder, with film-makers such as Peter Mullan, Danny Boyle, Lynne Ramsay, Dave McKay, playwrights such as Liz Lochhead, David Greig, Stephen Greenhorn, internationally respected graphic novelists like Grant Morrison, and even JK Rowling and Ian Rankin (creators of Harry Potter and Inspector Rebus, respectively) and many, many others who could have swelled and multiplied even this short list of names, have spearheaded a cultural revolution which continues to sweep through Scotland. In the worlds of music and the visual arts, bands like Primal Scream, Belle & Sebastian and Travis, alongside artists like Peter Howson, Caroline McNairn, and Alison Watt, are only the tip of an equally big iceberg. All have combined talent with integrity.

That is no mean achievement in a world where talent, like everything else, has been turned into a commodity to be bought and sold. There are many scriptwriters today churning out formulaic Hollywood blockbusters who have the capacity to write literary masterpieces. There are artistic geniuses galore in the advertising industry who spend their lives churning out elaborately constructed lies on behalf of shareholders they have never seen.

But a much bigger waste of talent is the talent that never sees the light of day. Our education system, for example, is heavily geared towards exams. From primary school right up to university, the emphasis is on regurgitating information fed down from on high rather than on developing creative skills. Unlike the sons and daughters of the rich, few working-class children ever get the chance of individual tuition from experienced painters or musicians or writers. Often, whatever creative impulses they display as young children become stifled and eventually suppressed as they progress through an education system in which teachers are forced to battle it out daily in front of large classes with sparse resources and little back-up.

One of the most precious commodities of all is time. Life is short; yet we spent a ludicrously large proportion of our lives doing things that we don't really want to do. It is an irony that some people from working-class backgrounds eventually develop talents that they would never have otherwise cultivated, such as writing, painting, musicianship, and sculpture, while they are serving lengthy prison sentences.

One of the central priorities of 21st-century socialism will be to progressively reduce the length of the working week. The technology probably exists even now on a European scale, if a proper inventory and assessment could take place, for a one-or two-day maximum working week across the board. Of course, such a step could not be taken overnight. It would require European-wide co-operation. It would involve a massive reorganisation of economic life and a huge expansion of training and education to redirect people from the more mundane occupations to professions such as teaching, nursing, and medicine.

But, even in the short term, and even in a small country like Scotland, a socially designed economy could immediately slash the working week to 30 hours, and eventually move towards a 20-hour and a ten-hour working week as the rest of Europe began to move in the direction of socialism. This, in turn, would allow a flourishing of art, literature, music, sport, drama, film, and other creative activities which few people have any time to devote to in our workaholic society.

Instead of paintings and sculptures being hidden away in art galleries in the more upmarket end of town, they would be everywhere. Pedestrian precincts, shopping malls, railway stations, residential streets will probably be lined with works of art. Writers and musicians could be paid by society as a whole, rather than from the proceeds of their books and records, a system that discriminates in favour of those artists who are commercially successful. Success would no longer be gauged primarily by sales and profit.

Over time, there would even be a blurring of the distinction between artists and the rest of society. Reduced working hours, the creation of a radical new education system accessible to everyone throughout their entire lives, a major shift in emphasis towards art and culture would enable everyone to become an artist in one sphere or another.

But competition is an important driving force of all human activity, some people will argue. Would a socialist society not be in danger of suffering from a surfeit of co-operation? Would it not lack the competitive edge that encourages people to strive for improvement, that inspires them to reach higher?

That is a fair point. Under capitalism, competition is extolled as the most important virtue of all, and its role in the development of society exaggerated out of all proportion. Nonetheless, it would be equally wrong to bend the stick too far in the opposite direction. Football is a co-operative sport, but it is also competitive. Without co-operation and teamwork, a football team is ragged and ineffective. But without competition, the game would be pointless. Who would play or watch a sport in which every contest ended in a draw?

Socialism would not seek to abolish competition, but to channel it in a different direction. There are two types of competition: negative, unhealthy competition, which is about exploiting, humiliating, injuring, killing, or conquering your opponent; and constructive, healthy competition, which is about testing your skills and talents against those of others, and in the process raising everyone's standards.

Under capitalism there is little genuine healthy competition.

Rivalry between businesses involves the bigger, wealthier corporations driving their weaker competitors to the wall. Rivalry between nations involves bigger, powerful states grabbing resources and territory from their smaller neighbours.

Even sport under capitalism has become, at least at its highest levels, a grotesque self-parody. In Scotland, senior football tournaments are all but auctioned off and sold to the highest bidders, with economic inequality among the clubs ensuring that the average match is as absurdly imbalanced as a bullfight or a foxhunt. In a socialist society, there could be wholesale redistribution of footballing revenues from the wealthy elite to the poorer clubs, and widespread democratisation of the game through the establishment of trusts and co-operatives.

In society as a whole, competition, far from being suppressed, could be directed away from the accumulation of money and power into more constructive channels, such as music, sport, literature, painting, film-making, songwriting, sculpture, architecture, or photography. Sport and popular culture could be subsidised in a future socialist society as ballet, classical music, and opera are in this society.

The mini cultural revolution that has occurred in Scotland over the past decade or so provides us with a tantalising glimpse of the talent which could be developed on a much wider scale in a society that seriously encouraged artistry and creativity. A talented array of ground-breaking fiction writers, poets, painters, film-makers, sculptors, comedy writers, playwrights, songwriters, and musicians representing diverse genres, backgrounds, tastes, influences, and ideological outlooks have emerged to add vibrancy and colour to Scotland's once prison-grey cultural landscape.

Most great artists throughout history have been radical in outlook. Genuine art can never stand separate and apart from reality. Its principal task is to communicate something – an idea, an emotion, a story. Art which is merely about creating perfection of form, or music which is solely about producing pretty sounds is unlikely to gain respect. But artists can never be dictated to by the rest of society without the art itself becoming corrupted.

Socialism would encourage the development of art and culture without interfering with the work of the artist and without taking sides in controversies about which schools of art or literature are superior. In the inter-war period, Josef Stalin in the Soviet Union promoted a school of art known as 'social realism' or 'proletarian culture'. Books, paintings, poetry all routinely glorified the working class, preached class struggle, and denounced the bourgeoisie. By contrast, the socialist writer and revolutionary, Leon Trotsky, argued that 'Art must find its own road ... The methods of Marxism are not its methods ... The field of art is not one in which the party is called to command.'[1]

As technology develops, there would be even greater emphasis on the arts. Computers are already capable of dealing with intricate tasks that involve logic and reason. When it comes to performing complicated calculations, or retrieving or sorting data, electronic intelligence has left the human brain light years behind.

But what the human brain with all its subtleties of consciousness and subconscious *can* do that computers cannot is defy the laws of logic. Humans are not just intellects and physiques – they are complex emotional beings capable of experiencing and conveying passion, humour, rage, jealousy, sorrow, love, hatred, sympathy, and a range of other feelings that are the raw materials of art, poetry, literature and music.

Unless, like mainstream pop music or pulp fiction, it can make pots of money for big business, creativity is marginalised in today's society. The so-called 'higher arts' are jealously guarded by self-perpetuating elites, who treat classical music, ballet, opera, art, and poetry as their own private property, with the gates bolted and barred to prevent the uncouth masses gaining access. But in a socialist society, all forms of art and entertainment will become an integral part of day-to-day life for everyone.

No-one can foretell at this stage exactly how socialism will evolve decades and generations into the future. As the French revolutionary Auguste Blanqui once said, 'Tomorrow does not belong to us.' Those who inherit socialism will shape it and mould it themselves, in accordance with the needs of future generations. All we can say for sure is that a new democratic economic system will usher in a revolution in culture, art, sport, morality, human relationships, everything.

Education, using the most advanced computer technology, would be open to everyone, with no age limits or restrictive hours. Other aspects of society could also be transformed. The philosophy of 21st-century socialism will be essentially libertarian. Capitalism combines economic libertarianism with social authoritarianism. Its power structures protect the right of big business to do exactly what it pleases, how it pleases, when it pleases. Yet ordinary people are subjected to masses of petty rules, regulations, and restrictions.

Someone caught in possession of a few grammes of a relatively harmless drug such as cannabis can be sent to jail; yet the owners of giant factories which churn out cigarettes or super lager, which cause death and misery on a mass scale, are rewarded with wealth, honours, and status.

Socialism in the 21st century will be the opposite of capitalism: it will combine economic regulation with social libertarianism. Everyone accepts the need for laws and law-enforcement agencies. No responsible person would oppose laws against drunk driving, or laws against mugging, or laws against racist attacks, or laws against rape, or laws against child abuse. But a new socialist Scotland could sweep away oppressive laws such as the current anti-trade-union laws, which are the most repressive in all of

Europe. It could remove from the statute books legislation such as the Criminal Justice Act, which seeks to criminalise people on the basis of their lifestyles.

It could overhaul the drugs laws, introducing controlled legalisation of relatively harmless soft drugs while treating hard-drug abuse as a medical and social problem rather than as a criminal offence.

It could democratise the legal system from top to bottom. The £150,000 judges, who, in the words of the writer William McIlvanney, 'are as removed from the lives of the working class as the Dalai Lama', could be replaced by elected panels representative of the real world.

In a future socialist society, even the human personality itself is likely to change over the course of generations. In today's world, values such as greed, selfishness, and ruthlessness are extolled, or at least tolerated, because the people who shape the moral atmosphere have themselves risen to the top by behaving greedily, selfishly, and ruthlessly. In a future socialist society, virtues such as co-operation, generosity and solidarity would become the values most admired.

Human relationships would no longer be forced into traditional straitjackets. Attitudes and behaviour that are regarded as 'natural' in one society are often denounced as 'unnatural' in another. Genuine socialism would be a society of independent citizens all free to choose their own lifestyle. It would promote tolerance and celebrate diversity rather than forcing people to conform. In all spheres of human activity, the emphasis of 21st-century socialism will be on individual freedom on personal matters, combined with collective decision-making on the wider problems of society.

In 1909, in his classic book, *Penguin Island*, the writer Anatole France exposed the sham of 'equality before the law' in a class-ridden society. 'The law, in its majesty equality, forbids the rich as well as the poor to sleep under bridges, to beg in the streets and to steal bread.'

Similarly, the 'freedom of choice' which we are all supposed to enjoy under capitalism is phoney to the core. Sure, we're all free to choose how we live our lives. We can choose to live in a detached mansion, or in a two-bedroom council flat. We can choose to eat in the Malmaison restaurant, or in Burger King. We can choose to develop our artistic, literary, or musical talents, or spend a third of our waking lives working in a job we don't even like.

For a privileged minority, these choices are real. For the vast majority, they are a mirage. Indeed, for billions of poverty-stricken people across the world, even the idea of living in a council flat, eating in Burger King, and working in an office would appear like nirvana.

Like a plant that has been deprived of water and light, the human personality has never yet had the chance to flower to its full potential. While society is shaped by the power of money, it never will. But, in the classless socialist society of the future, every human being will at least be allowed the opportunity to develop their skills, talents, and intelligence, and to live life to the full.

Chapter Twenty-one

HISTORY WITHOUT END

IN *CLOUD HOWE*, the second part of Lewis Grassic Gibbon's classic inter-war trilogy, *A Scots Quair*, the vision of 4000-year-old standing stones set against swirling clouds inspires the central character, Chris Guthrie, to think about the nature of time and change. The clouds that were once worshipped as gods, she thinks to herself, 'are just clouds, they passed and finished, dissolved and were done, nothing endured but the Seeker himself and the everlasting hills'.[1]

Gibbon himself was an uncompromising socialist. As a philosophical Marxist, he knew that even the 'everlasting hills' would not endure. Nothing is permanent or infinite. Mountains, islands, seas, species, planets, solar systems come into being, change, and eventually disappear.

In nature, changes tend to be measured in millennia. By comparison, human society evolves at breakneck speed. Yet how often do we hear people say: 'This is the way it's always been. There's no point in trying to change things.' Because our lifespan is short, we often find it difficult to see the big picture. We imagine that capitalism is immortal because it's been around for a few hundred years, which is tantamount to the blink of an eyelid when measured against millions of years of human existence. Yet, for many otherwise intelligent people, the system we live under today represents the final finished expression of civilisation. As the celebrated capitalist philosopher Francis Fukuyama puts it in his book, *The End of History*, capitalism is 'the final form of human government'.[2]

Over and over again, the idea is drummed into our heads that capitalism is the natural order of civilisation and that ideals such as socialism, co-operation, and egalitarianism go against the grain of human nature. Selfishness and greed is deeply embedded in our genes, runs the argument, backed up in literature by books such as William Golding's *Lord of the Flies*, where a group of boys marooned on an island revert to a Darwinian struggle for power culminating in the establishment of a ruthless hierarchy. Even the self-proclaimed socialist writer HG Wells wrote, 'The theory of natural selection . . . has destroyed, quietly but entirely, the belief in human equality which is implicit in all the "liberalising" movements of the world.'

All of this is mumbo-jumbo. Of course there are plenty of examples of greed and selfishness, but there also lots of examples of generosity and self-sacrifice. Most people are neither purely good nor purely evil, neither purely selfish nor purely altruistic, neither purely social nor purely antisocial, but are all of these things jumbled together. Every day millions of people donate blood, put money into charity tins, console friends in distress, look after ageing neighbours, devote precious time to voluntary work, and generally act in a fashion that is the opposite of the behaviour depicted in *Lord of the Flies*.

It is true that we are, partly at least, a product of our genes, and genes exist for no other purpose than to survive and replicate themselves. But, as the acclaimed genetic scientist, Richard Dawkins – who even wrote a book called *The Selfish Gene* – has repeatedly explained, natural selection favours those genes that are able to co-operate with other genes. Indeed, when co-operation between genes breaks down, death and destruction occurs. And, in any case, as Dawkins himself forcefully argues, genes can't think, they are mere molecules. Brains, on the other hand, which have been created from genes, *can* think and can consciously decide which social structures would be in the best interests of the majority of the population.

This argument about capitalism being in tune with human nature is an astonishingly enduring red herring. It overlooks the rather relevant fact that the earliest societies were organised on a communal basis. This wasn't because the ancient tribesmen and women were more egalitarian than their descendants; it simply reflected the fact that resources were so scarce there was nothing extra to siphon off.

If a member of a hunting tribe managed to kill a wild boar, he couldn't hoard it for himself or his immediate family. There were no deep-freezes in those days, so the hunter shared the spoils of the whole tribe on the understanding that, if someone else killed a large animal the next time, that too would be shared. The tribe also naturally co-operated with one other because that was the most efficient way to organise hunting and to ensure a steady supply of food.

What comes naturally – co-operation or rivalry – depends upon what is in the best interests of the majority in any given society. In different types of society, different value systems prevail. For example, in nomadic tribes, compulsory euthanasia of the elderly, the sick, and the frail was regarded in the past as natural. These tribes were forced to live a nomadic lifestyle because of the lack of vegetation in barren desert regions. Those who were elderly or infirm could not travel without imposing an intolerable burden on the rest of the tribe. And, no doubt, people living in these nomadic tribes imagined that compulsory euthanasia was part and parcel of human nature and would continue forever.

People have always found it difficult to rise above their immediate surroundings and visualise anything new or unfamiliar. Back in the Dark Ages, if anyone had suggested to our cave-dwelling ancestors that one day we would be living in gigantic cities with street lights and cars and telephones, they would have been laughed at.

When Spartacus led a slave uprising in Ancient Rome 2000 years ago, there would have been voices of common sense telling him that he was wasting his time. 'C'mon, Spartacus, get a grip! There's always been slavery. It's human nature to have slaves and slave-owners, and you can't change human nature!'

Throughout human history, there have always been people who cling to the past. Usually, but not exclusively, these are the people with wealth and power. They fear change, they resist progress, they grow nervous when confronted with ideas that are new and unfamiliar.

There are other people who thrive on change. They live, not in the past, or even in the present, but in the future. They refuse to worship before the altar of tradition. They challenge, and sometimes even break, the rules.

Nicolas Copernicus, for example, rewrote the rules of astronomy and was denounced from every pulpit in Europe because he challenged the universally accepted truth that the Earth was the centre of the Universe and everything else revolved around it. Beethoven rewrote the rules of music. Shakespeare rewrote the rules of literature and even morality. Napoleon rewrote the rules of warfare. Picasso rewrote the rules of art. Darwin rewrote the rules of biology. Newton rewrote the rules of physics.

Every great advance that has ever been achieved in art, science, literature, or music has depended upon people of vision and courage who have been prepared to stand up to the prevailing orthodoxies. At the start of the 21st century, the idea of a new social system based on equality, co-operation, solidarity, and democracy requires a certain leap of the imagination because such a society has never yet been built.

Most people are neither hidebound conservatives nor swashbuckling revolutionaries. They would rather settle for an easy life and leave the hard thinking to others. And that's exactly what they're encouraged to do by the people in power – because the more that ordinary people start to think things out for themselves, the more likely they are to challenge the status quo. 'If it ain't broken, don't fix it' is the guiding philosophy of many people. That's fair enough. But the social system we live under *is* broken and it's beyond repair. It can only be replaced.

Throughout history, there has been a whole succession of different social systems. Ancient tribal societies made way for slavery, which in turn was replaced by feudalism. All were progressive in their time. But they eventually ceased being progressive and were overthrown because they began to act as obstacles blocking the way forward.

Sometimes elements of the old system continued to co-exist alongside the new. Many of the Highland clans continued to operate a form of primitive communism after feudalism had conquered the Lowlands; slavery was only abolished in the United States towards the end of the 19th century; and the remnants of feudalism still exist in the United Kingdom today in the form of the monarchy, the House of Lords, and the landed aristocracy. But the general trend has always been for society to progress from a lower stage to a higher stage as it develops economically.

In its time capitalism represented a revolutionary leap forward. It challenged outdated traditions, smashed aside the rigid hierarchical structures of feudalism, and paved the way for the explosive development of science and industry. Without the overthrow of feudalism, the world's population today would be a fraction of its present size. Billions of people alive today would never have been born, because the technical means could never have been developed under feudalism to support such a large population. And of course, there would be no electricity, no motor vehicles, no air travel, no railways, no telephones, no computers, no TVs, no hypermarkets.

Many people, especially the capitalists themselves, claim that capitalism still plays a progressive role. They acknowledge that the system can suffer periodic booms and busts, upswings and downswings, recessions and recoveries. They even admit that the system creates gross inequality. But they insist that, for all its flaws, it does deliver the goods. Even if economic growth is punctuated with interruptions from time to time, the curve is climbing steadily upwards. So how can capitalism possibly be written off as an impediment to progress?

From the standpoint of pure economics, pure statistics, pure quantity of production, these claims have some validity. In terms of sheer quantity, capitalism today produces ten times as much as it did in the middle of the 20th century. It's also true that almost every day, especially in the field of computer technology, we see new innovations. But economic and technical progress no longer automatically equates with social progress.

For thousands of centuries, the basic task of humankind was to control nature and increase the productivity of labour. The invention of primitive tools, then more sophisticated tools, then machines, then large-scale industry all led to increases in production which benefited society as a whole. Of course, some people benefited much more than others; in parts of Africa today, economic progress might as well have halted some time back in the Middle Ages for all the impact it's had on the lives of ordinary people.

Nonetheless, as a general rule, economic and social progress historically marched forward hand in hand. But now the relationship has broken down. Under capitalism, the couple have drifted apart and gone their separate ways.

At least when the old-style industrialists introduced new techniques to maximise their profits, these technical advances tended to have spin-off benefits for society as a whole. Early capitalism was forced to develop a basic education system to ensure that people could cope in an industrialised urban environment. It was forced to provide public transport, public housing, basic medication, sanitation. Living standards and conditions steadily improved and working hours were gradually reduced.

Of course these improvements were not graciously handed down from on high by the capitalist owners of industry; they had to be fought for. Moreover, countries like Britain benefited from the imperial plunder of Africa and Asia. But technological progress did enable capitalism to concede reforms.

Today, technology enables capitalism to dismantle reforms. It is used to force down wages, increase hours, and destroy jobs. It is used by multimillionaires to hold national governments to ransom. It has created a massive surplus population – described by sociologists as 'the underclass' – which is forced to resort to the black economy, crime, and drug dealing in order to survive.

Capitalism may still be capable of economic progress. But the price of that progress will be even more environmental destruction, even more inequality, even more intensified, exploitation of labour, even more deregulation, even more anti-trade-union legislation, even more privatisation, even more unemployment, even more crime, even more violence. In other words, the price of economic progress in the 21st century will be social disintegration.

There is now a mind-boggling imbalance between the fantastic possibilities of social progress represented by new technology, and its ruinous consequences in practice for those sections of society excluded from the information revolution.

At this stage many people are fearful of change. The idea of tearing down the walls of capitalism and constructing a brand-new society on different foundations is a daunting prospect. Socialism seems like a gigantic leap in the dark. Isn't it better to stick with the devil you know?

That may seem like an easy option for many people right now. Like Harold MacMillan back in the 1950s, today's politicians tell us we've never had it so good. The economy is booming, although by the time you read these words, the boom may have turned into a recession or something even more severe. Like the Scottish weather, capitalism is a highly volatile system. Today's sunshine can turn into tomorrow's storm.

But, for the moment, let's give the economists the benefit of the doubt. Let's concede that the laws that have governed capitalism from its inception have been abolished, or at least temporarily suspended. Let's suppose there are no downswings, recessions, crashes, or slumps anywhere on the radar screen, and consider the best capitalism has to offer after 200 years of progress.

On the positive side, technology has provided millions in the wealthiest countries with a reasonable standard of living. Many of us are able to afford TVs, videos, central heating, microwave ovens, cars, computers, dishwashers, the occasional holiday abroad. In Scotland, as in most other Western European countries, we still have a welfare state, a National Health Service, and free education for all children. Not as good a welfare state or NHS as we used to have, mind you, but at least they still exist.

On the negative side, we have mass destitution in the Southern Hemisphere, where most of the world's population live. Indeed, the global north-south wealth gap has more than doubled over the past 50 years. Wars and ethnic barbarism engulf whole tracts of our planet. A nuclear arsenal has been developed which is capable of wiping out all human, animal, and plant life. Environmentalists warn of imminent global catastrophe.

In the rich countries, people are plagued by anxiety and insecurity. They live in constant dread of what tomorrow might bring. Many of us are up to our ears in debt. Our job is not as secure as it once was. We work long hours and have little time to ourselves. Working women with families live in a state of perpetual exhaustion. In our rural communities, increasing numbers of farmers are driven to suicide because of debt, poverty, and bankruptcy. In our cities, crime, drug abuse, alcohol abuse, child abuse, and domestic violence run rampant. Homeless people beg on our street corners. Our pensioners are worse off today than they were 20 years ago. Asthma among our children escalates to epidemic levels as the air we breathe becomes more and more poisonous.

And this is capitalism on a good day. This is capitalism after a decade-long upswing which is being hailed by the economists as 'an economic miracle'. This is capitalism at its most confident and optimistic.

'I'll tell you what I want, what I really, really want' sang the Spice Girls at the height of their fame in the late 1990s. But what do people really, really want? A few years ago, an organisation called the Women's Communication Centre carried out the largest ever survey of women's opinion. They asked tens of thousands of women the simple question 'What do you want out of life?'

A number of answers were repeated over and over again by thousands of women. They wanted clean air. A more equitable society. Time to do all the things they always wanted to do. Enough money to pay the bills, feed and clothe the children, and have a reasonable standard of living without constantly worrying about debt. Freedom from the drudgery of housework. Good health. Better working conditions. A shorter working week. A better education for their children. Access to education for themselves. An end to wars. An end to starvation. Peace of mind. Freedom from fear. Better public transport. More smiling faces. A happier world. More public celebration. Toleration. The right to live their own lives without being dictated to by others. A house with physical space and a garden.[3]

In this day and age, these demands are perfectly reasonable. Yet, as things stand right now, they appear unrealistic. That's because we suffer from stunted vision and poverty of the imagination. We can't end starvation in the Third World, we can't reduce the working week, we can't provide an adequate minimum wage, we can't provide decent housing for everyone, because the accountants who run the system on behalf of the rich tell us that we can't afford these things.

The truth is, all of these things and much, much more can be achieved by organising society differently. 'Imagine all the people sharing the world,' sang by John Lennon 30 years ago. 'Imagine all the people living life in peace.'

'But this is utopianism!' shriek the conservatives and the conformists. Oscar Wilde once issued a sharp retort to those who lacked the imagination to contemplate the possibility that things could be different: 'Show me a map without Utopia on it, and I'll show you a map that's not worth looking at.'

In the middle of the 15th century, Thomas More wrote a book called *Utopia*, in which he set out a vision of a society in which all property was socially owned. Contrary to popular mythology, modern socialism does not call for the abolition of personal property. Nonetheless, in some respects, More was half a millennium in advance of his time.

In the last four and a half centuries, there has been such a colossal development of science, industry, agriculture, education, and culture that the idea of common ownership, of egalitarianism, of the brotherhood and the sisterhood of man and woman is no longer utopian or absurd. What is absurd *is* the idea that the economic system we live under today will go on until the end of time.

Politics should be more than a series of petty squabbles between rival parties who share an identical, narrow vision of society. It should be about ideals and principles, philosophy and morals, economics and history, values and beliefs. This book does not lay any claim to political infallibility. The ideas set out here are not tablets of stone. Their purpose is to provoke a wide-ranging ideological debate the length and breadth of Scotland, and further afield.

Some of the detailed arguments set out here will no doubt be picked over like fishbones and criticised. But the key question is this: Which side are you on? Private greed or social need? Profits or people? Inequality or fairness? Hierarchy or democracy? Capitalism or socialism?

Notes

Chapter 1

1 *Daily Record*; December 31, 1999.

2 Scotland Against Drugs press release, December 29, 1999.

3 Statistics compiled from 1999-2000 annual reports from Scotland's major banks and insurance companies.

4 G. Stent, *The Coming of the Golden Age: A View of the End of Progress*, New York: Natural History Press, 1969.

5 Address to World Bank annual meeting, 1973. Quoted in 'Millennium Lottery', a report published by Christian Aid in 1999.

6 World Bank Report on development indicators, April 2000.

7 Human Development Report 2000, UN Development Programme, June 2000.

8 The figure of £750 billion was widely quoted in the business press at the time of the Asian financial crisis. If anything, it is an underestimate of the current volume of financial trading on the world's stock exchanges.

9 Statistic quoted by Jean-Francois Richard, Vice President for Europe of the World Bank, in 'Judgement Day for Our Brave New World', *Scotland on Sunday*, June 23, 2000.

10 George Kerevan column, *The Scotsman*, May 10, 1999.

11 Malnutrition Advisory Group report, January 7, 2000.

12 Report by Director of Development and Regeneration Services, Glasgow City Council referring to school year 1998–99 (undated).

13 *New Internationalist* magazine, March 1999.

14 Royal Society of Medicine conference on depressive illness, November 3, 1999.

15 For a full discussion see Joseph Rowntree Foundation report, December 9,

1999. See also, Susan Flockhart, 'Dear Sick Place', *Sunday Herald*, February 7, 1999 and Ian Bell, 'What Has Labour – Old or New – Done for Glasgow?', *The Scotsman*, December 17, 1999.

[16] Quoted in Brian Lewis, 'Poverty City', *Scottish Socialist Voice*, issue 1, vol. 2, October 23, 1998.

Chapter 2

[1] *Sunday Times'* Rich List 2000, *Sunday Times*, March 19, 2000.

[2] D. Peters et al; *Health Expenditure, Services and Outcomes in Africa 1990-96*: World Bank; 1999.

[3] *Newsnight*, October 17, 1999.

[4] Speeches to CBI conferences, November 1999 (Byers) and November 1995 (Blair).

[5] Although there is no officially recognised poverty line in the UK, charities such as the Child Poverty Action Group set their own definition of poverty, usually based on 50 per cent of average earnings after housing costs. The latest figures available were published in October 1999 and show one in four of the UK population – 14 million people – living in poverty. This compares with one in ten of the population – 5 million people – in 1979. From Child Poverty Action Group information document, 'Poverty Facts and Figures': CPAG 2000.

[6] Nigeria GDP figure from CIA 'World Factbook', 1999.

[7] *Sunday Times'* Rich List 2000, 'Scotland's Richest 100'.

[8] Ibid.

[9] Survey conducted for *Prospect* magazine by Centre for Economics and Business Research Ltd; October, 1995.

Chapter 3

[1] P. Murray, 'National Health Scandal', *Scottish Socialist Voice*, issue 22, vol. 2, January 21, 2000.

[2] *Chicago Tribune*, September 6, 1999.

[3] Report from chief economist at Merrill Lynch, *Washington Post*, August 7,

1997. Quoted in Stephen Haseler, *The Super-Rich: The Unjust New World of Global Capitalism*, Basingstoke: Macmillan Press, 2000.

[4] R. Lawrence, *Single World, Divided Nations? International Trade and OECD Labour Markets*, Paris: Brookings/OECD, 1996.

[5] J. Rifkin, *The End of Work: The Decline of the Global Labor Force and the Dawn of the Post-Market Era*, New York: Tarcher/Putnam, 1995.

[6] See Ian Angell, *The New Barbarian Manifesto (How to Survive the Information Age)*, London: Kogan Page, 2000. See also *LSE* magazine, Summer 1995 and 'The Smiling Prophet of Social Doom', *Scotland on Sunday*, December 31, 1995.

[7] See Alan McCombes, 'Scotland Needs Socialism', *Scottish Socialist Voice*, issue 1, November 22, 1996.

[8] See 'The Price of Success: Beyond the Great Worklife Debate', a report compiled by Ceridian Performance Partners and *Management Today*, 1999.

Chapter 4

[1] See J. Reid, 'John Buchan and the Legacy of Racism', *The Herald*, January 4, 1996. (Reprinted in J. Reid, *Power Without Principles: New Labour's Sickness and Other Essays*, Edinburgh: B&W, 1999).

[2] T. Gallagher, *Glasgow The Uneasy Peace: Religious Tension in Modern Scotland*, Manchester: Manchester University Press, 1987.

[3] Statistics from CWI (Committee for a Workers International) statement to commemorate International Women's Day, March 2000.

[4] F. Engels, *Origins of the Family, Private Property and the State*, 1886.

[5] J. MacLeod, *Highlanders: A History of the Gaels*, London: Hodder and Stoughton, 1996

[6] Information supplied by Campaign Against Domestic Violence.

[7] Information supplied by Gingerbread and One Plus.

Chapter 5

[1] See 'Benefits Butcher', *Scottish Socialist Voice*, issue 6, vol. 2, February 12, 1999.

[2] T. O'Boyle, *At Any Cost: Jack Welch, General Electric and the Pursuit of Profit*, New York: Knopf, 1998.

[3] *The Scotsman* business section, February 16, 2000.

[4] *The Scotsman* Business 300, March 1996.

[5] *Fair Trade Yearbook 1994*; *New Internationalist*, August 1998; *New Internationalist*, September 1995; *New Internationalist*, October 1999.

[6] John Lloyd column, *Scotland on Sunday*, January 23, 2000.

[7] *The Times*, September 17, 1999.

[8] Tony Blair, Prime Minister's Question Time, April 5, 2000.

[9] J. Gray, *False Dawn: Delusions of Global Capitalism*, London: Granta, 1999.

[10] Ibid.

[11] I. McWhirter, 'Labour Rushes In Where Thatcher Feared to Tread', *Sunday Herald*, November 14, 1999.

[12] Gray, *False Dawn*

Chapter 6

[1] M. Friedman, *New York Times*, September 13, 1970. Quoted in J. McMurtry, *The Cancer Stage of Capitalism*, London: Pluto, 1999.

[2] Ibid.

[3] C. Wolmar, *Stagecoach: A Classic Rags to Riches Tale from the Frontiers of Capitalism*, London: Orion, 1998.

[4] *Business Week*, July 18,1997.

[5] Ibid.

[6] G. Soros, *The Crisis of Global Capitalism*, New York: Public Affairs, 1999.

[7] J. Seabrook, 'Hands Without Bodies', *New Internationalist*, July 1996.

[8] P. McGill, *Children of the Dead End*, London: Caliban, 1982 (first published 1914).

[9] *The Hollow State*, BBC2, 1996.

[10] B. Brookes and P. Madden, *The Globetrotting Sports Shoe*, Christian Aid,

1995. Also for more recent information, see the Nikewatch website at www.caa.org.au/campaigns/nike.

11 N. Rufford, 'Prisons to Offer Telesales Jobs', *The Times*, August 10, 1997. According to this article, Tony Blair was considering implementing a similar scheme in British prisons.

12 J. Gray, *False Dawn: Delusions of Global Capitalism*, London: Granta, 1998.

13 Sir Donald MacKay, 'Nothing Must Stand in the Way of Free Trade's Global March', *Scotland on Sunday*, December 26, 1999.

14 M.J. Mandel, 'The Risk that Boom Will Turn to Bust', *American Business Week*, February 14, 2000.

Chapter 7

1 See website, *Who Owns What: The Database of Media Ownership (General Electric Corporation Overview)* at www.mediaownership.org/ge

2 Inland Revenue Statistics 1999.

3 J. Paxman, *Friends in High Places*, Harmondsworth: Penguin, 1991.

4 See T. Benn, *The Benn Diaries 1940-1990*, London: Hutchison, 1995.

5 P. Taaffe, T. Grant and L. Walsh, 'The State: A Warning to the Labour Movement', Militant Pamphlet, 1983.

Chapter 8

1 E.J. Hobsbawm, *The Age of Revolution: Europe 1789-1848*, London: Cardinal, 1973.

2 See Douglas Rushkoff, 'Breaking the Tech Myths (Before they Break Us)', November 1998; and 'The Shareware Universe' (undated), www.rushkoff.com

3 T. O'Boyle, *At Any Cost: Jack Welch, General Electric and the Pursuit of Profit*, New York: Knopf, 1998.

4 A. Einstein, 'Why Socialism?' was published in the *Monthly Review*, New York, May 1949.

5 *New Scientist*, June 30, 2000.

6 Figures provided by US-based cancer research charities.

[7] I. Pearson, 'Our View of the Future (The Future of Capitalism)', British Telecommunications plc, 2000. This can be downloaded from the following web address:

www.bt.com/innovation/viewpoints/pearson/capitalism.htm

[8] Ibid.

Chapter 9

[1] J. McMurtry, *The Cancer Stage of Capitalism*, London: Pluto Press, 1999.

[2] Statistics provided by the Hadley Centre, linked to the UK Met Office.

[3] See 'Climate Change and its Impacts' (Kyoto, 1997; Buenos Aires, 1998; Bonn, 1999), Hadley Centre.

[4] *The Ecologist*, March/April 1999.

[5] L. McDonald and A. Myers, 'Malign Design', *New Internationalist*, November 1998.

[6] S. George, *The Lugano Report*, London: Pluto Press, 1999.

[7] S. George, *How the Other Half Dies*, London: Pluto Press, 1986.

[8] McDonald and Myers, 'Malign Design', *New Internationalist*, November 1998.

[9] I. Bell, 'Are Our Farmers Doomed?', *The Scotsman*, September 15, 1999.

Chapter 10

[1] A. Wightman, *Who Owns Scotland*, Edinburgh: Canongate, 1996.

[2] T. Johnston, *Our Scots Noble Families*, Glendaruel: Argyll Publishing, 1999 (New Edition).

[3] Wightman, *Who Owns Scotland*.

[4] A. Cramb, *Who Owns Scotland Now?*, Edinburgh: Mainstream, 1996.

[5] Jan van de Ploeg appeared on the programme on October 19, 1995. Quoted in Wightman, *Who Owns Scotland*.

[6] Royal Bank of Scotland Monthly Oil and Gas Index.

[7] C. Woolfson, J. Foster and M. Beck, *Paying for the Piper; Capital and Labour in Britain's Offshore Oil Industry*, London: Marshall, 1996.

[8] Quoted on *Wasted Windfall*, Channel 4, September 18, 1994.

[9] G. Brown, ed., *The Red Paper on Scotland*, EUSPB, 1975.

[10] *Petroleum Economist*, August 1998.

Chapter 11

[1] Glasgow Corporation Water Works archives, Glasgow University Library.

[2] J. McMurtry, *The Cancer Stage of Capitalism*, London: Pluto, 1999.

[3] *Scotland on Sunday* business section, February 13, 2000.

[4] McMurtry, *The Cancer Stage of Capitalism*.

[5] M. Sawyer and K. O'Donnell, *A Future for Public Ownership*, London: Lawrence & Wishart, 1999.

[6] Ibid.

Chapter 12

[1] Speech to Labour Party Conference, 1996.

[2] From H. McDiarmid, 'A Drunk Man Looks At The Thistle', 1926.

[3] Labour General Election Manifesto, February 1974.

[4] W. Hutton, 'Greed is Good, Too Good to be True', *Observer*, January 30, 2000.

[5] J. Gray, *False Dawn: Delusions of Global Capitalism*, London: Granta, 1998.

[6] *Observer*, September 29, 1996.

Chapter 13

[1] From Tony Blair's keynote speech, March 28, 2000.

[2] John MacLean, (Scottish Workers Republican Party candidate, Gorbals constituency), Election Address, 1922.

[3] See Royal Bank of Scotland Monthly Oil and Gas Index.

[4] Royal Bank of Scotland Economics Office Report, March 20, 2000.

[5] George Kerevan, *The Scotsman*, August 16, 1999.

[6] George Kerevan, *The Scotsman*, June 24, 1999.

Chapter 14

[1] B. Brecht, *The Solution*, 1953.

[2] Quoted in *John MacLean*, Nan Milton, London: Pluto Press, 1973.

[3] For more information about the economic achievements of the USSR, see Roger Silverman and Ted Grant, *Bureaucratism*, or, *Workers Power*, Militant, 1975.

[4] See *Forbes* magazine articles on Russia, September 7, 1998; November 16, 1998; March 22, 1999.

[5] *Revolution Betrayed* by Leon Trotsky was first published in 1936. It is now out of print, though it is worthwhile trying to get a second-hand copy of this seminal analysis of totalitarianism in the Soviet Union.

Chapter 15

[1] T. Bunyan, *The Poltical Police in Britain*, London: Quartet Books, 1983 (first published in 1975).

[2] See E. Truman, 'Hacked Off', *Scottish Socialist Voice*, issue 16, vol. 2, September 30, 1999.

[3] S. Milne, *The Enemy Within*, London: Verso, 1994.

[4] I. Roxburgh, P. O'Brien and J. Roddick, *Chile: The State and Revolution*, London: Macmillan Press, 1977.

[5] Quoted in Milne, *The Enemy Within*.

[6] The Zapatista website is at www.ezln.org

Chapter 16

[1] Quoted in T. Sheridan and A. McCombes, 'Struggle, Solidarity and Socialism', Scottish Militant Labour pamphlet, 1994.

[2] Inland Revenue Statistics 1999.

[3] The findings were published in *The Scotsman* in November 1998.

[4] A. Neil, 'Walking With Ideological Dinosaurs', *The Scotsman*, November 12, 1999.

Chapter 17

[1] 'British Social Attitudes Survey 1999', conducted by National Council for Social Research.

[2] See G. Orwell, *Homage to Catalonia*, Harmondsworth: Penguin, 1989 (First published 1938); H. Thomas, *The Spanish Civil War*, Harmondsworth: Penguin, 1977; Sam Dolgoff, ed., *The Anarchist Collectives: Workers' Self-Management in the Spanish Revolution 1936-39*, Free Life Editions, 1974.

[3] See C. Doyle, *Month of Revolution: France 1968*, Fortress Books, 1988. See also reports in *Sunday Times* by Patrick Searle and Maureen McConville, May 1968.

[4] J. Foster and C. Woolfson, *Politics of the UCS Work-In: Class Alliances and the Right to Work*, London: Lawrence & Wishart, 1986.

[5] C. Woolfson and J. Foster, *Track Record: The Story of the Caterpillar Occupation*, London: Verso, 1988.

Chapter 18

[1] W. Ferguson, *Scotland's Relations with England: A Survey to 1707*, Edinburgh: The Saltire Society, 1994.

[2] The poem 'Sic' a Parcel of Rogues in a Nation' is by Robert Burns.

[3] A. Gray, *Why Scots Should Rule Scotland*, Edinburgh: Canongate, 1997.

[4] P. Berresford Ellis and S. McA'Ghobhainn, *The Scottish Insurrection of 1820*, London: Gollancz; 1970.

[5] N. Milton, *John MacLean*, London: Pluto, 1973.

[6] A. Marr, *The Battle for Scotland*, Harmondsworth: Penguin, 1992.

[7] J. Cannon, 'From Karl Marx to the Fourth of July', *The Militant*, reprinted in *Notebook of an Agitator*, New York: Pathfinder Press, 1973.

Chapter 19

[1] These figures derive from calculations based on statistics from *The World Factbook 1999*, Central Intelligence Agency, United States, and from J. Peat and S. Boyle, *An Illustrated Guide to the Scottish Economy*, London: Duckworth, 1999.

[2] S. Flockhart, 'Dear Sick Place', *Sunday Herald*, February 7, 1999.

[3] M. Sawyer and K. O'Donnell, *A Future for Public Ownership*, London: Lawrence & Wishart, 1999.

[4] See Scottish Socialist Party conference document, 'The Scottish Economy: Scotland's Economic Gulf'. The figure was calculated by dividing the combined profits made by overseas companies in Scotland by the number of Scottish employees on their payroll.

[5] Peat and Boyle, 'An Illustrated Guide to the Scottish Economy'; company annual reports 1998-99.

Chapter 20

[1] See I. Deutscher, *The Prophet Unarmed: Trotsky 1921-1929* (vol. 2 of a 3 vol. biography of Leon Trotsky), Chapter III, 'Not By Politics Alone', Oxford: Oxford University Press, 1959.

Chapter 21

[1] L. Grassic Gibbon, *A Scots Quair*, vol. 2, *Cloud Howe*, Edinburgh: Lomond, 1986.

[2] F. Fukuyama, *The End of History and the Last Man*, Free Press, 1992.

[3] The 'What Women Want: Values and Visions' survey was conducted throughout 1995 by the Women's Communication Centre.

Bibliography

All texts referred to in the endnotes are included in this bibliography, together with some selected additional material.

Benn, Tony, *Arguments for Democracy*, London: Cape, 1981

Benn, Tony, *The Benn Diaries 1940-1990*, London: Hutchison, 1995

Brookes, Bethan and Madden, Peter, *The Globetrotting Sports Shoe*, Christian Aid, 1995

Brown, Gordon, ed., *The Red Paper on Scotland*, EUSPB, 1975

Bunyan, Tony, *The Political Police in Britain*, Quarter Books, 1983

Callendar, Robin, *How Scotland is Owned*, Edinburgh: Canongate, 1998

Cannon, James, *Notebook of an Agitator*, New York: Pathfinder Press, 1973

Cocks, Martin and Hopwood, Bill, *Global Warning*, London: Militant Publications, 1996

Cramb, Auslan, *Who Owns Scotland Now?*, Edinburgh: Mainstream, 1996

Davies, Norman, *The Isles*, London: Macmillan, 1999

Deutscher, Isaac, *The Prophet Unarmed: Trotsky 1921-1929* (vol. 2 of a 3 vol. biography of Leon Trotsky), Oxford: Oxford University Press, 1959

Devine, T.M., *The Scottish Nation: 1700 to 2000*, Harmondsworth: Penguin, 1999

Doyle, Clare, *Month of Revolution: France 1968*, London: Fortress Books, 1988

Einstein, Albert, *Why Socialism?* can be downloaded from the website of the Socialist Party of Orlando at www.socialistpartyoforlando.freeservers.com

Berresford Ellis, P. and McA'Ghobhainn, S., *The Scottish Insurrection of 1820*, London: Gollancz, 1970

Engels, Friedrich, *Origins of the Family, Private Property and the State*, Various, 1886

Ferguson, William, *Scotland's Relations with England: A Survey to 1707*, Edinburgh: The Saltire Society, 1994

Fukuyama, Francis, *The End of History and the Last Man*, New York: Free Press, 1992

Gallagher, Tom, *Glasgow the Uneasy Peace: Religious Tension in Modern Scotland*, Manchester: Manchester University Press, 1987

George, Susan, *How the Other Half Dies*, London: Pluto Press, 1986

George, Susan, *The Lugano Report*, London: Pluto Press, 1999

Gibbon, Lewis Grassic, *A Scots Quair*, Edinburgh: Lomond, 1986

Gray, Alasdair, *Why Scots Should Rule Scotland*, Edinburgh: Canongate, 1997

Gray, John, *False Dawn: The Delusions of Global Capitalism*, London: Granta, 1998

Haseler, Stephen, *The Super-Rich: The Unjust New World of Global Capitalism*, London: Macmillan Press, 2000

Hobsbawm, E.J., *The Age of Revolution: Europe 1789-1848*, London: Cardinal, 1973

Hutton, Will, *The State We're In*, London: Vintage, 1996

Kelman, James, *Some Recent Attacks: Essays Cultural and Political*, Edinburgh and San Francisco: AK Press, 1992

Lynch, Michael, *Scotland: A New History*, London: Pimlico, 1992

McGill, Patrick, *Children of the Dead End*, Caliban, 1982

MacLeod, John, *Highlanders: A History of the Gaels*, London: Hodder and Stoughton, 1996

McMurtry, John, *The Cancer Stage of Capitalism*, London: Pluto Press, 1999

Marr, Andrew, *The Battle for Scotland*, Harmondsworth: Penguin, 1992

Marx, Karl and Engels, Friedrich, *The Communist Manifesto*, Various, 1848

Milne, Seumas, *The Enemy Within*, London: Verso, 1994

Milton, Nan, *John MacLean*, London: Pluto Press, 1973

Nairn, Tom, *The Break Up of Britain*, London: Verso, 1981

Nairn, Tom, *Faces of Nationalism: Janus Revisited*, London: Verso, 1997

Nikewatch website at www.caa.org.au/campaigns/nike

O'Boyle, Thomas, *At Any Cost: Jack Welch, General Electric and the Pursuit of Profit*, New York: Knopf, 1998

Roxborough, Ian, O'Brien, Philip, Roddick, Jackie, *Chile: The State and Revolution*, Basingstoke: Macmillan Press, 1977

Orwell, George, *Nineteen Eighty-Four*, Harmondsworth: Penguin, 1949

Orwell, George, *Homage to Catalonia*, Harmondsworth: Penguin, 2000

Paterson, Lindsay, ed., *A Diverse Assembly: The Debate on a Scottish Parliament*, Edinburgh: Edinburgh University Press, 1998

Paxman, Jeremy, *Friends in High Places*, Harmondsworth: Penguin, 1991

Pearson, Ian, 'Our View of the Future: The Future of Capitalism', British Telecommunications plc, 2000. This can be downloaded from www.bt.com/innovation/viewpoints/pearson/capitalism.htm

Peat, Jeremy and Boyle, Stephen, *An Illustrated Guide to the Scottish Economy*, London: Duckworth, 1999

Pilger, John, *Hidden Agendas*, London: Vintage, 1998

Prebble, John, *The Highland Clearances*, Harmondsworth: Penguin, 1963

Reid, Jimmy, *Power Without Principle: New Labour's Sickness and Other Essays*, Edinburgh: B&W, 1999

Rosenberg, Chanie, *Nineteen Nineteen*, London: Bookmarx, 1987

Sawyer, Malcolm and O'Donnell, Kathy, *A Future for Public Ownership*, London: Lawrence & Wishart, 1999

Scottish Socialist Party Conference 2000; 'Scottish Socialist Party Policy 3 Statements and Resolutions', 2000

Sheridan, Tommy and McAlpine, Joan, *A Time to Rage*, Edinburgh: Polygon, 1994

Soros, George, *The Crisis of Global Capitalism*, New York: Public Affairs, 1999

Stent, Gunther, *The Coming of the Golden Age: A View of the End of Progress*, New York: Natural History Press, 1969

Taaffe, Peter; Grant, Ted; and Walsh, Lynn, *The State: A Warning to the Labour Movement*, Militant Pamphlet, 1983

Trotsky, Leon, *Revolution Betrayed*, Various, 1936

Who Owns What: The Database of Media Ownership at www.mediaownership.org/ge

Wightman, Andy, *Who Owns Scotland*, Edinburgh: Canongate, 1996

Williamson, Kevin, *Drugs and the Party Line*, Edinburgh: Rebel Inc, 1997

Wolmar, Christian, *Stagecoach: A Classic Rags to Riches Tale from the Frontiers of Capitalism*, London: Orion, 1998

Woolfson, Charles, Foster, John and Beck; Matthias, *Paying for the Piper: Capital and Labour in Britain's Offshore Oil Industry*, London: Mansell, 1996.

Young, James D., *The Very Bastards of Creation*, Glasgow: Clydeside Press, 1995

PERIODICALS

The Ecologist, London; Monthly

International Socialist, Dundee; Quarterly

Links, Australia; Quarterly

New Internationalist, Brighton; Monthly

New Scientist, London; Weekly

Red Pepper, London; Monthly

SchNEWS, Brighton; Weekly

Scottish Socialist Voice, Glasgow; Fortnightly

Socialism Today, London; Monthly

Statewatch, London; Bi-monthly

Index